THE CHANGING FACE OF CHILDHOOD

By the same author

The Changing Face of Beauty
Fashion

The little girl who holds up her drawing
with such delight lived in the early
sixteenth century, but both she and her picture
could be of the present day.
'Fanciullo con Pupazetto', by Caroto.
Double view of a little boy's head by Tchilicheff

MADGE GARLAND

The changing
face of
childhood

HUTCHINSON OF LONDON

Hutchinson & Co. (*Publishers*) Ltd
178-202 Great Portland Street, London, W.1
London Melbourne Sydney Auckland Bombay
Toronto Johannesburg New York

First published 1963

© Madge Garland 1963

Designed by Jane Mackay

*The energetic small boy does not appear to be
hampered by his long skirts and fine feathered hat.
'The Little Gardener', by J. S. Copley*, R.A.

This book has been set in Bembo type face.
It has been printed in Great Britain on White Coated paper
by William Clowes and Sons Ltd, London and Beccles, and bound by them.

To my goddaughter Colombe

CONTENTS

The prime symbol of Christianity:
a beautifully gentle example of the Florentine School
which shows a loving Mother and a plump Babe,
their hieratic haloes faded to a faint nimbus.

ILLUSTRATIONS

The child as Eros: Third century.
Graeco-Roman boy's head

The darling young

Inevitably any conception of childhood must be a false one since it cannot be described by the child himself but is only a reflection of what the adult imagines he remembers. Every individual and each age sees the child differently: at various times regarded as a symbol of fertility, a gift of God, the spawn of Satan, a valuable pledge in power-politics or a heavy financial burden, these disparate concepts have been reflected by artists and writers of all ages – but the chubby child remains remarkably the same. The small Greek girl hugging her pet, the little second-century Egyptian boy threatening never to speak to his father again unless he is brought a coveted gift, the cries of fear or pain, the plea for food – these could be of any age. It is the outward conditions and the attitude of the adult which change rather than the child himself.

It is almost impossible to realize today that once upon a time children were considered of little account and, paradoxically, in a

*The child as an idol:
the Santo Bambini of
St. Maria in Aracoeli
is entirely robed
in jewelled offerings.*
RIGHT: *As a fertility symbol
Archaic statuette of mother
and child in terra cotta.*

sparsely populated world were ignored and ill-treated while now, when a rapidly expanding birth-rate poses unanswerable problems, the claims of all children of every class and colour, whole or handicapped, are allowed – perhaps in expiation of the many crimes committed against them in the past.

As a fertility symbol the child is common to all civilizations. Some of the earliest-known frescoes and artifacts in the world are mother-and-child figures connected with fertility rites, the belief in whose efficacy has survived throughout the centuries in the many harvest rice-maidens and corn-dollies which in some remote countries are still made to ensure the fecundity of the crops. For the same reason some ancient societies buried children under their dwelling-houses.

In classical times a laughing child was a symbol of sexual love and as Eros became the prototype of countless cherubs who later lost all individuality until the 'putti' became a mere decorative convention.

The myth of Cupid clearly tells that the god was both willing and able to undertake the rôle of a man; David's neo-classic painting, showing a lovely youth – said to be a portrait of the then American minister's son – about to step naked out of Psyche's bed, as clearly illustrates the story.

The child was inconspicuous in both the art and literature until, long after the foundation of Christianity, the Church abandoned the Christ-Pantocrator as prime symbol of the faith and replaced it by the Mother and Child. It is in the arms of the Virgin that the child

A sombre Mother holds her man-Child, hieratic symbols of a severe faith. Both figures are heavily draped, their heads encircled by stiff haloes. Russian Icon.

*Renaissance pictures of
the young were of real
living children, no longer
symbols of sex or religion.
'The Christ Child
and St. John'. Botticelli.*

enters the realm of art. From that time to this the myriad facets of
maternal love have been an inspiration to artists of every age, and the
child a subject of interest.

The stiffly draped manikins of the early icons which sad-faced
Virgins hold on their knees and the children of the Old Masters are
rarely childlike, but gradually a great change came about, the dark
draperies disappeared, the heavy halo became a glittering nimbus, the
crowned and bejewelled Virgin a human woman, the doll-figure a
real child. The babe underwent a series of metamorphoses, the pale
rickety infants of the early Flemish masters gave place to Botticelli's
fine champion children, palpably nourished on a different diet as well
as the products of a more genial civilization. The loving Mother playing with her beautiful Child is a picture of life's possible happiness,
not a sad emblem of humanity's certain suffering. The anomaly of
the Mother worshipping her own Babe – 'en effet, comme c'est
drôle, cet enfant qu'elle partage avec Dieu', wrote Claudel – is one
that never surprises, only pleases.

*Blake asks 'What is Man?'
and compares the swaddled child to
the caterpillar grub.*
RIGHT: *Domenico di Bartolo's
swaddled babe being given to its
foster-mother recalls a chrysalis.
Detail from 'Nurture and Marriage
of the Foundlings'.*

But in spite of the cult for the Mother and Child small importance
was attached to real children. Medieval pictures and stories of them
are few: Chaucer's 'lytel clergeon' trailing his coat in the ghetto and
steadfastly singing the song which later gained him a sainthood, is a
rare exception. Children had no rights of their own, from the moment
they were born their limbs were bound as tight as any mummy, and
as they grew up all freedom of thought and action was restricted by
severe discipline. No matter how brutal, frivolous or indifferent their
parents might be the child was taught he owed them complete
obedience and a great debt of gratitude for having produced him,
whereas the present climate of opinion, even among the most harum-
scarum parents, is more often one of apology for bestowing the
questionable and unasked gift of life.

Past generations thought little of exercising their power to end that
gift: Iphigenia and Andromeda were both offered up, and Isaac
narrowly escaped being a sacrifice. The widespread habit of exposing
unwanted or deformed infants in a lonely spot and leaving them to
die continued in Greece until the time of Plato. Indeed it was still
practised in the last century when Mary Kingsley found a compatriot

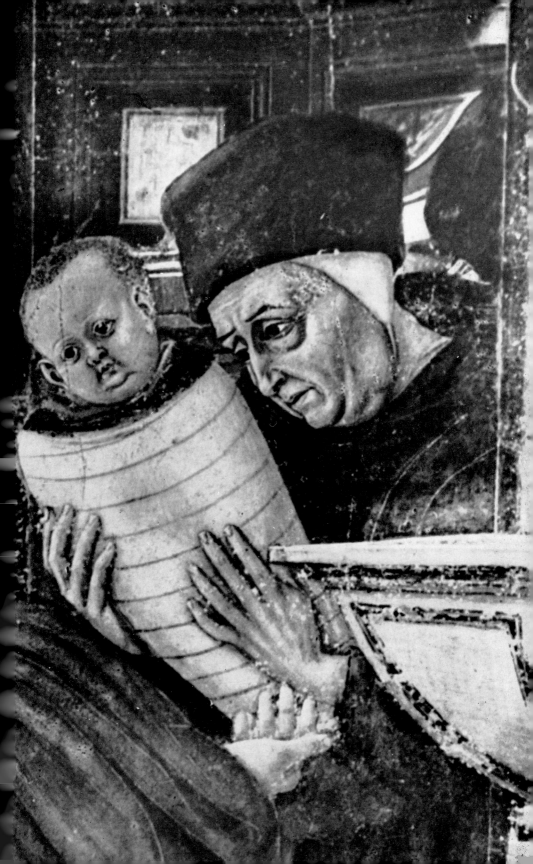

Henry Moore's exquisitely happy mother and child in bronze, and RIGHT: *an Australian Aboriginal pre-history fresco which illustrates the same theme.*

20

succouring such babes in the forests of West Africa. Little girls, always less in demand in a harsh world which preferred warriors or hunters, were frequent victims and few people in any period would have agreed with Sydney Smith who said 'I am glad it is a girl: all little boys ought to be put to death'. Yet individual parents in the past must have loved their children just as they do today, David's grief was great over his sick baby, both Hector and Andromache bewailed Astyanax, and the feelings of the babies' mothers were accurately assessed by Solomon when he gave his judgement.

An immense revolution of thought has taken place within the last hundred years. Parents have been deposed from their Olympian heights and their power diminished; compelled to combine the functions of playmates and dictators, they often find themselves, Janus-wise, uneasily facing both ways at once. Children are no longer chattels but have special privileges of their own. Today there would be a legal remedy against a father's action such as Trollope deals with in *He Had to be Right* where a husband, separated from his wife because he erroneously believed her to be unfaithful, will not allow her to see their child unless she confesses and repents. As she is innocent she cannot do this, and her friends are extremely worried about her, yet there is no concern for the year-old boy himself, abandoned to a landlady and then taken abroad with an unknown nurse, whereas now the child would be the first concern of all.

Nor were children in the past considered attractive: the conception of the young as universally appealing is a modern one. A seventeenth-century writer refers to the 'repugnance' aroused by the sight of a child, and many earlier civilizations drastically tried to alter what nature had given them. Races as dissimilar in time and culture as the ancient Egyptians, the Eskimos and the American Indians all admired

LEFT: *The infant face, once considered repugnant, later became a source of inspiration to painters and sculptors alike.* 'Peggy Ann', *by Epstein.* RIGHT: 'Baby in Red Chair', *by unknown American primitive painter.*

*The Cholmondeley Sisters in their stiff ruffs and boned bodies are
as straitly confined as their poor babes, capped and wrapped
in lace-edged lawn and heavy brocade. English School.*

an elongated or cone-shaped head and a whole arsenal of contraptions
existed which attempted to improve on nature by compressing the
infants' heads into peculiar shapes.

The child remained an anonymous actor in the wings of its parents'
life until the Reformation unfortunately raised the issue of original
sin. Nowhere did the shadow of Calvin lie more darkly than over the
nursery, he declared that the whole nature of children was a 'seed bed
of sin' and that only by whipping could their inherent wickedness be
eliminated and their salvation ensured. Bunyan described children as

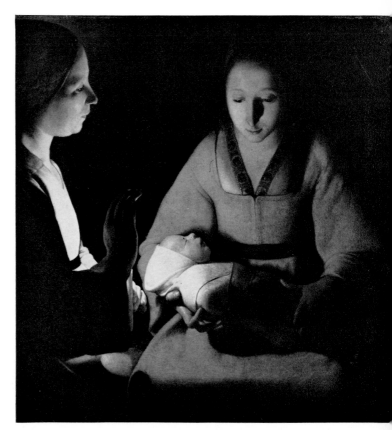

*Limbs and head tightly bound
the New Born Child is illumined
by Georges De La Tour's magical lighting.*

'cursed creatures', Puritan manuals demanded 'What was thou being an infant but a brute, having the shape of a man? what is youth but an untamed beast?' A more moderate author wrote to a child 'I would fain do what I can to keep thee from falling into everlasting fire' and encouraged him with a tale of a 'very serious ... child who had a comfortable Death when he was 12'. 'Death – I wish it weren't called that ... I don't think I should mind it so much if it were called Hig' said Pamela Glenconner many years later, when most of the hell-fires had been extinguished.

The consciousness of death and hell impressed on children in their early infancy appals a generation which has dropped the word 'Hell' from the Prayer Book: happily no little girl today would remark, while looking at herself in the mirror, 'What a pity such a pretty maid as I should go to Hell', nor would any parent cross-question his sick child as to whether he would rather live or die. No wonder a little boy so pestered replied he would rather go to God, 'because I love God'. What a world away is Jowett's remark to Margot Asquith, 'My dear child, you must believe in God in spite of what the clergy tell you!'

But a gentler and more humane way of life was growing and John Earle could write 'a child is purely happy because he knows no evil'. The shadows were lightening. Traherne could see the boys and girls

At a time when high infant mortality was usual, few families can have been as fortunate as the Father and Sons and Mother and Daughters so delightfully painted by Bartholomeus de Bruyn the younger.

playing in the streets as 'moving jewels' and say that 'Adam in Paradise had not more sweet and curious apprehensions of ye world than I when I was a child'. Even so, few children recalled their childhood with the same nostalgia as Vaughan who wrote 'Happy those early days when I Shin'd in my angel infancy', or could say with Thoreau 'I can remember that I was all alive, and inhabited my body with inexpressible satisfaction'. Far more seem to have been like poor Mary Coleridge who describes her young self as a 'dumb unliving child' scarcely able to 'recall anything except the sharp sensations of fear that broke the dull dream of my days'. The thread of FEAR runs through most accounts of children's lives, fear of God, of their parents, of hell, of hunger, of being whipped, of the dark, of cold baths, a fear of 'hobgoblins, Boneless and such other Bugs', and a hundred other bogies. Yet now that most of these have been removed from the modern child, fear still remains. Many still wonder, even if they do not ask

'Are all the dragons fled?
Are all the goblins dead?
Am I quite safe in bed?'

and await the answer of

'You are quite safe in bed
Dragons and goblins all are dead.'

Some children, like Julian Green, felt that to frighten others and to frighten himself was a breathtaking delight, but the awful hours he spent each evening on the staircase, too afraid of the dark above to go to his bedroom, made so deep an impression on him that in his novels a darkened staircase often leads to a painful incident. Forrest Reid admitted his fear of the dark was so obsessive that nightmares of it haunted him until he was 10 years old. He endeavoured to conquer this cowardice by appealing to God, but was deeply grateful to his eldest sister who would leave the sitting room door ajar and sing loudly in order to

The dark and cluttered interiors of the past were full of possible goblins and ghosts to the imaginative child. 'Un Coin d'appartement'. Claude Monet.

28

Romantic security: the Roi de Rome asleep in a woodland, by Prud'hon.
Realistic security: a child asleep in the Underground during London's Blitz.
Henry Moore.

LEFT: *Peace and plenty,
generous curves and warm
colour; Madame Renoir
with her son Pierre,
by Renoir.*
RIGHT: *Poverty,
grey paint and
the kitchen sink.
Jack Smith.*

give him courage. The 'fields and roomy chambers of memory' are full of childish anguish and too often the child's exuberance is mistaken for happiness. As Lord Berners pointed out, 'black care can sit behind a rocking horse'.

The child lives in two worlds, that of his own making and that of the adults who surround him, and the immense rôle played by the imagination in his life cannot be over-estimated: in Francis Thompson's happy phrase 'the universe is his box of tricks'. Jane Taylor said when she was reading romances she lived so much in a castle that she forgot she lived in a house, and the Brontë children writing their Gondal stories were far from their bleak parsonage.

More than any other poet or painter Blake was able to translate the visions of the child into the language and iconography of the adult. Familiar with God from the age of 4 when he saw the holy Face looking in at him from the window of his house in Soho Square, by 10 accustomed to seeing angels – once a tree was so full of them that their bright wings 'bespangled every bough like stars' – he had no difficulty in realizing the child was a part of heaven.

A hundred years later another great writer of innocence, Francis

Thompson, understood that poet and child belonged to one species
and could write unself-consciously

> 'Little Jesus, wast Thou shy
> Once, and just so small as I?...
> Hads't Thou ever any toys,
> Like us little girls and boys?'

Such glimpses of pristine innocence did not greatly influence art and
though a special limelight is thrown on children by such artists as
Chardin, Reynolds and Renoir, most pictures of them are worldly
and factual. But while little Victoria was growing up in obscurity the
nineteenth century began to discover 'little children', and 'the darling
young', as Francis Thompson called them, seemed as if they had come
into fair waters at last. Two women of genius gave lasting expression
to what, alas, was to be a fleeting moment. Berthe Morisot and Mary
Cassatt were supremely able to convey the radiant and fulfilled love
of the mother and the child's touching unawareness of its warm and
sheltered happiness. They never guessed that an unknown Viennese

*The 'Master Baby' pictured by Sir William Orchardson at
the turn of the century is palpably loved and pampered.*

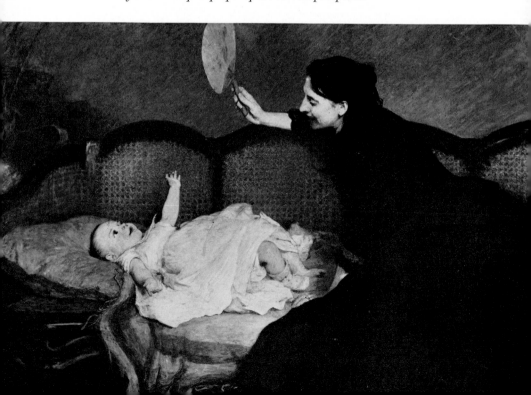

*Mary Cassatt's touching Mother and Child recall W. B. Yeats's
tender cradle song 'I kiss you and kiss you, My Pigeon, my own;
Ah, how I shall miss you When you have grown'.
Modern parents appear to have quite different feelings
towards 'Le Nouveau Né'. Bernard Buffet.*

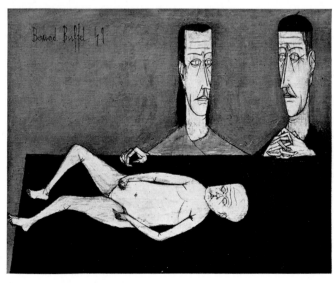

In 1898 all the traffic of Piccadilly could be halted for His Majesty the Baby. In all probability the little boy in white satin trimmed with white marabout would be killed in World War 1. Arthur Drummond.

professor was soon to prove their recently found innocence a sham. Baby dear, out of the sky so blue, and that 'Tiny alabaster girl Hardly bigger than a Pearl' were discovered to be monsters of such iniquity that even Calvin and Bunyan might have been surprised to discover just how right they had been. If Swinburne saw a baby as a 'very rose of roses' and Francis Thompson described a small girl as a snowflake, Freud used quite other similes. Horrified parents, to whom the rod was now taboo, began to wonder if they were encouraging an

Oedipus complex when they kissed their children good-night. Should they merely shake hands? Should the children be shielded from believers in storks and gooseberry bushes as firmly as their ancestors had segregated Catholics and Puritans? The child who hitherto was considered bad and was beaten, was now diagnosed as badly integrated and sent to be analysed. If given the choice between birch and couch might he not have preferred the one more quickly over? In the past infants were taught about death and sin, now they were instructed in sex and no sin – often with strikingly little success, as when John Gunther explained the human sexual habits to his 3-year-old son, who replied 'Oho, you can't fool me – that's too funny to be true' ...

Between the sad past of original sin and the sad present of endemic sex the brief moment at the end of the last and the beginning of this century, when all traffic could be held up for His Majesty the Baby, appears a golden age when children had emerged from their long centuries of oppression, were cherished and believed to be innocently lovely, an interlude of normal happiness when simple questions brought simple answers:

> What does the bee do? Bring home honey.
> And what does Father do? Bring home money.
> And what does Mother do? Lay out the money.
> And what does Baby do? Eat up the honey.

An extreme example of unrealistic childhood: decorative rococo Putto on a Dolphin, from Berg-am-Lain.

East or West a child's first lesson is in prayer. Three small figures from the Chinese Scroll of a Hundred Children.

Their learning

The first words children of whatever denomination or colour have learnt to speak, apart from the local variant of mama or papa are, or were, words of prayer. Almost as soon as the infant could walk – or even before – it was taught to pray. Most of the young were admonished to learn their prayers by severe parental threats of hell-fire, few children were pursuaded as charmingly as the little girl to whom Matthew Prior wrote:

> 'My noble, lovely little Peggy
> Let this my first Epistle beg ye
> At dawn of morn and close of even
> To lift your heart and hands to heaven:
> In double duty say your prayer:
> Our Father first, then Notre Père.'

After prayers were mastered came lessons which in the past began far earlier than they do now. Children grew up young and were

A serious babe joins its hands in prayer. French School, fifteenth century.

ABOVE: *A tiny babe toddles uncertainly towards his Ayah. Tilly Kettle.*
LEFT: *A bandy-legged cupid who has learnt to walk too soon. Detail from 'Venus and Love'. Cranach.*
OPPOSITE: *The old-time method of teaching a child to walk by means of a moving cage has recently been revived. Detail from 'A Family Group'. G. Coques.*

Two details of the Portinari altarpiece, showing two boys and a girl kneeling in prayer. Van der Goes.

considered adult with their education completed at an age when modern scholars have barely left kindergarten. As late as 1200 'infancy endeth for both sexes' at the age of 7, when little boys became pages and little girls began to learn domestic lore.

Medieval lessons were concerned with manners rather than learning. The *Babees' Book*, one of the earliest known manuals for children, more suited to the tens than the twos – but the word 'baby' was then applied to a much older age than now – gives a vivid picture of a medieval child's up-bringing. It equates good breeding with a love of horses, hawks and armour, not with letters, and makes clear that a nobleman's son should be a valiant knight not a poor scholar. It lays great stress on good behaviour and on courtesy, then considered the basis of the social system, for it was said 'courtesy came to earth below when Gabriel hailed our Lady by name, and Elizabeth to Mary came', but makes no mention at all of actual learning. The instructions listed are those any mother gives to even the most delinquent modern child, i.e. not to pick his nose in public, not to talk with his mouth full and so on. 'How the Gude Wyfe taught her Daughter' what a well-brought up girl should know in the fifteenth century in England can be read in the long poem of that name, which also ignores all three R's. In contrast to education in classical ages, when Horace considered too much music and dancing demoralizing, it was more important for the medieval girl to dance and sing than to know her letters.

Most of the young acquired only the barest rudiments of learning and such opportunities as were offered the children of Charlemagne were rare. This great man, far in advance of his time, instructed the English monk Alcuin to give the same lessons in grammar, geography, astronomy, logic and moral philosophy to his daughters as his sons. Alfred the Great was equally fair to his family, but both kings wisely insisted the girls should also learn weaving and needlework. Such sensible ideas were not in keeping with feudal society whose chivalrous notions encouraged the seclusion of women, and the education of girls was greatly neglected. Little boys continued to be sent to noble houses to be trained as pages and later became squires to their lord, a habit which had its origin in the eleventh century when young hostages were held in castles taken by the Norman conquerors, and the systematic training of Saxon boys in Norman households was part of the conquerors' planned policy. At a later date Becket was often attended by a throng of as many as thirty boys whom he 'trained in honourable learning and accomplishments'. This tradition of sending the young away from home early has bitten deep into the English way of life and has had an immense influence on boys' upbringing.

In the far past girls were better educated than many nearer to us in time. The ancient cultures of Babylonia and Egypt must have given them a reasonably good grounding since they were permitted to manage estates, run a business and act as scribes in courts of law. The matriarchal system of Egypt in which landed property and royal authority descended in the female line, gave women considerable power and, presumably, sufficient education to manage their own affairs. In England it was not until 1882 that women were allowed to own property.

Some four hundred years lie between these two little boys reading, yet their poses are strikingly similar. LEFT: *The young Cicero, by Foppa.* RIGHT: *The artist's son. Picasso.*

Lessons began early in the past:
here the child Jesus, enchantingly attired in a pleated dress,
pretty bonnet and shoes, is being encouraged by his Mother
and a young John the Baptist. Carpaccio.

When Plato suggested girls should be trained on the same lines as boys nothing came of his ideas, but the sexes must have had fairly equal opportunities in classical Greece for we hear of girls competing successfully with men in poetical contests and Erinna, called 'the Bee', became a famous poetess before her death at the age of 19 – ten years older than her Scottish opposite number, Marjorie Fleming.

In most Roman families boys and girls were treated alike and together were taught letters from alphabets cut out of ivory, arithmetic by counting with pebbles, and to write with a metal stylus on a wax tablet. They seem to have been lured on to these achievements by sweetmeats and tartlets much as children today are by sugar-sticks and ices. Even then girls were not expected to reach quite such a high level as boys, for as they would not enter commerce or politics Greek was not essential, just as Latin until recently was obligatory for boys but not a regular part of the curriculum in girls' schools.

What education there was in Europe during the Middle Ages was entirely in the hands of the Church. The first school for boys in England was opened in the tenth century by Irish monks at Glastonbury, in 1394 Winchester was founded for 'poor scholars', Eton followed some fifty years later, and by the fifteenth century there were several which, with subtle social distinctions, catered 'for gentlemen's sons and other gude men's children'. These establishments gradually took the place of the noble families to which boys previously had been sent for training and as they were modelled on monastic foundations their rules were correspondingly severe. The 'litel childe his litel boke learning, As he sat in the scole at his primere' was holding in his hands a book named after that used by the monks and, like them, the scholars were expected to rise early and to recite a large number of daily prayers. The day began at 5 a.m. when they had to say their first prayer while making their own beds and they retired with their last prayer at 6 p.m. They were badly housed, poorly fed and frequently flogged and it is no wonder that some of their mutinies were so serious that they had to be put down by the Army. Most of them would have agreed with Thomas More's summing up of their plight:

'I am called Childhood: in play is all my mind
To cast a quoit, a cok-stele and a ball.
A top can I set and drive it in its kind:
But would to God these hateful bookes all
Were in fyer burned to powder small;
Then might I lead my life always in play.'

There was little time for play, there were no regular holidays and though there were many saints' days and religious feasts these became rarer after the Reformation, and the strange liberties accorded to the 'Boy-Bishop', who once a year took precedence of his elders and preached a sermon from the pulpit, were finally ended by Elizabeth. Echoes of some old customs still survive: the ceremony of giving new-comers to Eton a gift of salt, which later was distributed to the townspeople in exchange for money, is perpetuated in the name of Salthill now a suburb of near-by Slough, and Eton still has a Montem Road in memory of the Montem festivities which were only discontinued late in the last century.

There is now better food and regular holidays, Eton boys no longer make their own beds and have fewer prayers to recite, but these children of the rich endure conditions of hardship which no proletarian child would tolerate. The system of fagging (a word not used before the end of the eighteenth century, but which probably derives from the faggots for the fire which the smaller boys had to fetch for the bigger) still continued, though not with quite such brutal incidents as were previously only too common. This inexplicable method, which might as easily turn a boy into a sadistic tyrant as into an exceptionally understanding human being, is one of the major puzzles of the British way of life and is incapable of rationalization. One can only say – with reservations – that it works.

Foreigners have always been startled at the harshness of the English towards their young: a sixteenth-century Italian visitor decided that parents simply did not *like* their children, and a later traveller summed up the whole English public school system in two words, fagging and flogging. One boy wrote with feeling

'I would my Master were an hare,
And all his bokis howndis were!
And I myself a jolly hontere –
To blowe my horn I wold not spare!
For if he were dede I wold not care.'

Erasmus strongly condemned the brutality with which the boys were treated and wrote a work entitled *A declamacion that chyldren even strayt fro ... their infancie should be well and gently broughte up in learnyge.* But it was no good. The very emblem of teaching was the instrument of punishment, schoolmasters were always represented with a birch or rod, even a dame in her school is shown always with one before

*The indignity of whipping was never more clearly illustrated than in
this fresco by Benozzo Gozzoli in the church of St. Augustine, San Gimignano.*

*Learning the hard way in 1516: scholars seated on a wooden bench
or being taught their letters at a standing desk.
The master holds the inevitable birch. Ambrosius Holbein.*

47

her. How little boys must have envied Prince Edward, Princess Elizabeth's brother, who as a Royal stripling was allowed a 'whipping boy' to be beaten in his stead. A seventeenth-century writer recounts how a schoolmaster on a cold morning would whip pupils for no other reason than to get himself warm! Charles Lamb's description of the punishment meted out to the boys when he was at Christ's Hospital is appalling: the first time the miserable boy was *mis en fers*, the second put in a cell with only bread and water, and the third dressed as a fool and beaten before all the school. He and Erasmus would be pleased to know that in 1962 when a boy was sentenced to twelve strokes of the birch in Australia, the sentence was inoperative because there are no birch trees in that continent and legal advice held that an offence would be committed if twigs of any other tree were used to carry out the punishment. The mother-country was approached, whereupon consternation reigned in the Prisons Department because it was fifty years since the last birching took place and no birches could be found.

Tales of cruelty to little girls are, perhaps, less frequent, though poor Lady Jane Grey complained bitterly that she was 'so sharply taunted ... with pinches, nips and bobs ... that I think myself in hell till time comes that I must go to Mr. Elmer' (John Aylmer, her tutor), and the horrifying boarding school described so vividly in *Jane Eyre* was taken from a well-known establishment founded by a minister of the Church.

The liberal spirit of the Renaissance did much to encourage education in all classes regardless of sex. Parents began to dedicate their children to the muses, not the Church, and the 'golden boys and girls' of Mantua, Urbino and Ferrara combined the manners admired in the Middle Ages with the new love of learning, and excelled in dancing and hunting as well as belles-lettres. Their governess wrote revealingly of the d'Este children 'they are anxious to learn and EVEN to work'.

Across the Channel the first treatise on girls' education was written for Mary Tudor by order of her mother, Katherine of Aragon, described at 16 when she came to marry the Prince who was later Henry VIII, as 'the most accomplished princess ever to come to

The use of the globes was at one time considered part of a young lady's education. This rather puzzled little girl, wearing a magnificent pearl-embroidered dress, holds an astrolabe in her hand. Jan van Gossaert, called Mabuse.

England'. She caused this to be drawn up by an austere Spanish priest who forbade all books of chivalry or romance, permitted only a few classic poets, the Gospels and the works of the saints, but included the same homely detail which Charlemagne and Alfred insisted should be in their royal daughters' curriculum – that 'she was to learn to handle wool and flax, for the dressing of wool hath ever been an honest occupation for a woman', even if she were a Princess of England.

A few girls boarded at convent schools and some families sent girls as well as boys to noble households for experience and training. Bess of Hardwick went to stay with Lady Zouche in London to learn the art of cookery and the control of staff when she was 12, and had no time to lose for she was married at 13 to a boy of 15, but most little girls lived with and were taught by their elders. They were not yet relegated to nursery or schoolroom, but apart from household matters few learnt more than reading, writing and the elements of arithmetic, though some had tutors, mastered the globes, sang and played on the viol, while a few of high birth were immensely

The Blue-coat boys were for long one of the sights of the City. Here they form part of the picture entitled 'London Visitors', by J. J. Tissot.

studious. Gradually letters began to assume the status once held by manners. The story of Thomas More's three remarkable daughters is too well-known to be repeated, and perhaps Sir Thomas exaggerated as fathers are apt to do when he praised sweet Meg's 'so pure a stile, so good Latine', just as one has occasional doubts of the eulogies bestowed on Princess Elizabeth's learning, who was credited with Latin, French, Spanish, Italian and moderate Greek, but she was certainly the mistress of a number of languages at an exceptionally early age.

The sixteenth century was a period keenly conscious of its debt to classical learning and with a great longing to enlarge its mental attainments as well as its physical horizons. During the first Elizabeth's reign more schools were erected than all those which had existed previously, and it became possible for most would-be scholars to attend a neighbouring grammar-school. The vogue for French which dated from the Conquest and lasted to the seventeenth century began to decline, it no longer followed that 'Jack would be a gentleman, if he could speak French', a knowledge of Latin now became essential for any educated person. As the number of schools multiplied the merchant and professional families found they could be rid of their little brats while at the same time aping their betters, so remarking smugly that they were 'desyring nothing more thanne Educacion and bringing upp Chyldren in good Maners and Litterature' they despatched their small sons to one of the new schools. If the children were cold, hungry and beaten – well, they were being trained in the ways of human beings. The British Isles saw no counterpart of Montaigne père's experiment of placing his little boy in the care of a kind but humble family where he might enjoy plain food and a quiet life, and be awakened by the strains of music so that he should never be startled. These were, and are, far from the British point of view. But little Michel Montaigne was far ahead of the other children in his class when he went to school – and lived to write his *Essays*.

The London merchants of Elizabeth's reign founded schools connected with several of the city churches and guilds, some of which survive today. The Merchant Taylors', where the scholars were so well-known for their patriotism that they were called Loyalty's Bulldogs, is still a major centre of education for business men's sons though it is no longer in London. The most famous school was that of Christ's Hospital near Grey Friars, founded by Edward VI, whose scholars wore the costume of blue soutane held by a leather belt, white jabot and yellow stockings which made the 'Blue Coat' boys one of the sights of London for hundreds of years. Early in this century the school was moved to the country but the costume has never changed.

An hour-glass marks the passing of time for the poor elderly Dame and her bewildered scholars. John Opie.

After the Reformation education was no longer a prerogative of the clergy and

> 'In every village mark'd with a little spire,
> Embowered in trees, and hardly known to fame,
> There dwells in lowly shed, and mean attire,
> A matron old, whom we school-mistris name.'

A dame's school was now the fate of the very young, or of those whose family was too poor to send them to boarding school, and most hamlets boasted a small building

> 'Where a deaf, poor, patient widow sits
> And awes some thirty infants as she knits.'

The dame in charge is always shown in pictures as an elderly woman with a hook nose, spectacles, a shawl and a birch: she surely must have had more than one physical appearance, but no other has come down to us. In her day-school the mysteries of numbers and letters were expounded with the aid of a horn-book, a bat-shaped wooden slab on which the alphabet, the numerals and sometimes the Lord's Prayer were inscribed, the whole protected by a thin sliver of horn. This practical object, which was exclusive to England, later became a general term for any alphabetical table whether or not it was covered by horn. Some were quite elaborate, like little Princess Elizabeth's which had a frame of filigree silver and a fine leather mount, some had illustrations or were covered with talc, but the usual school-child's was a sturdy wooden affair which after lessons was also used for games such as bat and ball or shuttlecock. There are several portraits of children showing them attached by a cord around the waist or hanging from the wrist, and the term 'battledore boy' meant one who was learning his lessons. These sensible horn-books continued in general use until in the last century printed books became cheap.

An excellent device much appreciated by children for learning the alphabet was the gingerbread with raised letters which they could finger, learn and then eat. Some of these cakes, which continued to be made until the end of the last century, had gilt borders, hence the expression 'taking the gilt off the gingerbread', i.e. buying broken pieces.

The method of learning the alphabet by means of cubes with letters on them has been common for hundreds of years and still exists, but A for Archer in Elizabeth I's reign has become A for Astronaut in Elizabeth II's. Counting was sometimes taught by means of little crosses: the jingle 'And if you know the Christ-cross row You soon may spell and read' probably refers to the Cross shown at the beginning and end of the letters on the horn-book and has given us the word 'criss-cross'.

The dame lasted until Froebel transformed her into a 'children's gardener', one who taught exhilarating games in a kindergarten instead of words by rote when immobilized on a bench. But the birch, or some corporal punishment very like it, lingered on. Julian Green tells the extraordinary story of the teacher at his first school in Paris early in this century who, when she wished to punish a child, made him step up to her, then after she had beaten his knuckles with a rod, insisted he should kneel down and kiss her hand.

Schools multiplied in the seventeenth and eighteenth centuries but the standard was low and England lagged far behind France and Germany in educational matters. Queen Anne's learned friend Mary Astell tried to make her take an interest in the subject but to no avail, and curiously enough neither the Prècieuses Ridicules in France nor the Blue Stockings in England had much influence on children's education. Wretched foundlings in charity schools were firmly grounded in such articles of faith as the brevity of life and the dreadful fate in store for sinners and not much else; one sad little girl of 6 records on her sampler 'This have I done, I thank my God, Without

LEFT: *A Lavallière bow and a pom-pom topped beret were typical of the schoolboy when Renoir painted the young André Bérard in 1879.* OPPOSITE: *The now-rare black apron, once worn by all French school-children, is recorded in this sketch by Vuillard.*

correction of the rod'. The ordinary schooling of the middle classes was so bad that 'a girl which is educated at home with her mother is wiser at 12 than a boy of 16 who knows only Latin'; the lower classes were not educated at all, and upper-class girls continued to get a smattering of French and learnt to dance and embroider while their fashionable mothers passed their time gambling.

There were exceptions: in France Madame de Maintenon founded the convent-school of Saint-Cyr where over two hundred little girls wore the pretty costume, so singularly unlike the drab school uniforms of today, of blue cloaks over blue gowns, and lace-trimmed caps each tied with a coloured ribbon to signify their class. Selina Trimmer, the enlightened governess of the lovely Duchess of Devonshire's children, used the magic lantern to enliven their lessons – but then the Cavendishes, like the Gonzagas of two hundred years earlier, stand out in history as two groups of exceptionally favoured beings, vividly illumined by the light of their intelligence and beauty. Madame de Genlis also used the magic lantern to teach history, expounded botany during country walks and encouraged her royal pupils and little Pamela to make herbals of dried flowers and leaves such as Rousseau advocated, a craft which was later practised by most Victorian young ladies.

Madame Campan, who had been a reader to Louis x v's daughters and had started a small school at St. Germain in 1795, did not approve of Madame de Genlis's confused enthusiasms for new methods and preferred to turn out well-bred, sensible young people. Among her first pupils were a 12-year-old girl with dusky gold hair and her brother, sad children whose father had been guillotined. Later their mother remarried and their stepfather was so pleased with their deportment that he sent two of his own sisters to be educated by Madame Campan. The children's names were Beauharnais and Bonaparte and as one of them later became famous as Pauline Borghèse it is questionable, if morals not manners are borne in mind, whether Madame Campan's system was wholly admirable ...

At an earlier date a school for young gentlewomen in Chelsea had unwittingly become immortal through their master asking Henry

Purcell to provide the music for a pupil's performance. So it came about that the sublime lament of Dido when she bids Aeneas farewell was first sung by an unknown schoolgirl at an end of term concert – but then Racine wrote *Esther* and *Athalie* for the schoolgirls of St. Cyr, who were probably much as they are today, for a contemporary comedy included 'two tawdry, hoyden overgrown Romps of the Boarding School'. Any mother would recognize the description and they most likely differed little from those girls whom Aristophanes said were typical Athenians, 'always too late in everything they do'.

Learning slowly began to be of greater importance, even for girls, and although deportment was still considered vital, music and dancing were no longer the prime accomplishments of young ladies.

A dancing lesson in 1832: in the great hall
the children hold out their skirts and point their satin slippers,
watched by their admiring parents. C. R. Leslie.

When Hannah More was asked to draw up a plan for Princess Charlotte's education she went so far as to recommend that children should 'tussle with some parts of Mr. Locke's Essay concerning Human Understanding' – a quality in which she surely must have been deficient, though she did realize that the true aim of education was to teach a human being HOW he could teach himself.

The standard educational work of the early nineteenth century, referred to in a novel by Jane Austen, was *Mangnall's Questions*, the work of the 'Hammersmith Semiramis', as Thackeray called Miss Mangnall whose Select Establishment was the original of Miss Pinkerton's in *Vanity Fair*, probably the most famous school in fiction. A diary still exists written by a girl of that time which gives a vivid picture of the Question and Answer method then generally in use.

But the time for experiment had begun. In France Rousseau's educational schemes were considered visionary and had little immediate effect, but his ideas upset conventional thinking and laid emphasis on the claims of the child: an ideal in no way disturbed by practical experience as he deposited his own children – all illegitimate – in foundling homes. His belief in complete freedom and a total lack of discipline, which has borne strange fruit in this century, is illustrated by a contemporary picture which shows two naked infants wrestling on the floor, watched by their admiring parents. Beneath is written 'Voilà la règle de la nature, pourquoi la contrariez vous?' Many a modern parent could answer that apart from the possibility of the children catching cold, there was every probability of their becoming delinquents.

In Switzerland a movement to reform the up-bringing of children was begun by that great idealist Pestalozzi which is still in force today, and there is hardly a child who does not owe something to this great man who, though he failed to interest Napoleon in his plans, has succeeded with countless thousands of human beings since. Many of his ideas were put in a more practical form by Froebel, and kindergartens throughout the world bear witness to the imagination and true love which at last released the child from moral bigotry and physical fear.

In England an experiment of a different kind was carried out under the guise of philanthropy. It would bear quite another name today. Mr. Thomas Day, the author of that school classic *Sandford and Merton* in which snobbery is nauseatingly mixed with complacent priggishness, decided he would adopt two little girls and bring them up himself in order to see which was worthy of becoming his wife. One soon disappointed him and was apprenticed to a milliner. To the other he applied his 'novel principles', some of which consisted in teaching the child fortitude by firing pistols at her petticoats and dropping hot wax on her arms, telling her imaginary secrets to see if she were discreet, and teaching her to prefer a plain taste in dress. The result was that she had to be sent away to school and later given some money to marry someone younger and, we hope, more reasonable. Oddly enough Mr. Day's method of inculcating courage was not unique: the great-grandmother of someone still living was taken by her father into a churchyard where he fired a pistol at her petticoats so that she could learn not to be afraid – with excellent results. She grew up spirited and fearless: once when her coachman wanted to use a roundabout route to evade a district frequented by highwaymen, she put a pair of pistols into the man's back and forced him to continue on the main road, while her small son, continuing the family tradition of valour, cried 'Fire, mama, fire'.

Such individual and original methods became obsolete when the School Act of 1870 required all children to attend school. A die-hard of 1879 remarked ... 'which schooling We rate-payers must perforce afford To youth whom better-nurtured lads And lasses would describe as cads, And give an education That may unfit them for their station'. Nevertheless English schooling lagged far behind the highly proficient system whose minister said in 1846 'I promised God I would look on every Prussian child as a being who could complain of me before God if I did not provide him with the best education both as a man and as a Christian'. Although a system of national education had begun in England in 1834, schooling was not wholly compulsory for all until 1918.

Towards the end of the nineteenth century many girls' boarding schools were opened and though most schoolmistresses were similar to the one Henry James said, 'viewed her little pupils as so many small slices cut from the loaf of life on which she was to dab the butter of arithmetic and spelling, accompanied by way of jam with a light application of the practice of prize-giving', some began to provide a more serious curriculum. Girton was founded in 1869 and the famous Miss Buss and Miss Beale set a hitherto un-dreamt-of standard at the colleges they directed.

> 'Miss Buss and Miss Beale
> Cupid's darts do not feel
> How different from us
> Miss Beale and Miss Buss.'

These new centres of female learning inherited something of the austerity which characterized boys' schools of an earlier age, the severe

The small Eastern scholars look infinitely more orderly and better behaved than those in the West. Indo-Chinese class by Mai-Thu.
RIGHT: *A late nineteenth-century Infant School by Jean Geoffroy*

new buildings and their serious inmates contrasted strongly with the peacock courts and splashing fountains envisaged by Tennyson for his learned Princess.

In the years prior to World War I the ideals of nineteenth-century

reformers were developed by a brilliant Italian woman. Dr. Montessori's realization that the child would learn more easily from its own experiments and mistakes than from other people's theories and lessons, and her ingenious methods for awakening the mind and senses, have had an overwhelming influence on the teaching and daily life of the young all over the world.

During the reign of Elizabeth II an outburst of school-building, comparable to that which took place under the first Elizabeth, covered green fields with buildings of glittering glass. The number and size of the windows in these new schools would have appalled the conservative Tudor gentlemen who viewed with anxiety the buildings of such houses as Hatfield and Hardwicke, and predicted the rising generation would be blind before it was 40 from the perpetual glare in which it lived. But already in 1962 American architects were declaring that no windows at all were necessary: they pointed out that with new methods of building and ventilation no natural air or light was required. The hated class-room smell of ink, chalk, slate pencils and small persons was a thing of the past, modern systems of

The sorrows of childhood are much the same in any epoch:
BELOW: *The fifteenth-century little boys*
painted by Uccello weep and are afraid.
OPPOSITE: *The schoolroom is slightly hostile*
as it has always been. Lewin Bassingthwaite.
RIGHT: *The Victorian Naughty Child by Landseer*
has broken her slate and is put in a corner.

lighting, heating and air-conditioning guaranteed a perfectly clean atmosphere of even temperature and light-strength all the year round. The day-dreamer would no longer be able to look out on the passing clouds: divorced from all contact with unpredictable nature, might not children be made at last into predictable human beings?

In such antiseptic settings elegant manners are of no importance, morals not mentioned, music and dancing mere fringe activities and scientific learning is all. In Chaucer's time a captious critic had complained that 'every cobbler's son and begger's brat goes to school now-a-days' – what would he have said to A level examinations and the Red Brick Universities?

These new standards of education presuppose a late age development in singular contrast to the precocity so much admired in the past. Earlier periods not only expected children to behave like grown-ups but credited them with adult emotions. Floris, King of 'Spaygne', and his Blancheflour were said to have fallen in love with each other when they were 7, Dante with Beatrice when both were 9. John Evelyn deplores the marriage of Lord Arlington's daughter, the 'sweetest, hopefullest, most beautiful child', to a 'rudely bred' boy but was not shocked because she was 5 and her bridegroom 9. Both Catherine de Medici and her bridegroom were 14 when they married but were so much in love that the little 'reinette' and her boy-husband used to go away into corners with their arms round each other. The Dauphin who later became Louis XIII was married in the full sense of the word when no older as the diary of the court physician, Heroard, leaves no doubt. One of Edward I's daughters was 5 when she made her profession as a nun; Matilda, William the Conqueror's daughter, was 8 when she was praised for her good manners at her coronation as Empress of Germany; two Renaissance girls both achieved fame before they were 14 – Trivulzia of Milan as a Latin orator, and Olympia Morata of Ferrara as author of an Apologia of Cicero. Evelyn's son was only $2\frac{1}{2}$ when he could read English, French, Latin and Gothic letters, Thomas Cowley had his poems printed when he was 10, at 7 Thomas Lawrence was already painting portraits. That horrid child, Anna Seward, later known as the Swan of Lichfield, lisped *L'Allegro* and *Il Penseroso* when only 3, her eyes swimming with delight (any nannie nowadays would have called it showing off, but then she was greatly admired). Princess Charlotte at the same age, burlesquing the way in which Mr. Canning took off his hat and tearing her cap into shreds while she recited 'How doth the little busy bee' to Hannah More, seems in every way a more endearing figure.

The tradition of precocious children was carried on into the nineteenth century by little Marjorie Fleming who, at the age of 6, decided that as she was no longer a baby she would learn and write a great deal of poetry. Sir Walter Scott delighted to carry his 'pet Marjorie' wrapped in a Scotch plaid sewn up at one end like a

Time for a music lesson in Victorian England;
the geranium stands on the lace-covered table,
the lid of the fretwork-decorated piano is open. J. Collinson.

65

shepherd's, to the literary salons of Edinburgh where she entertained the company by reciting poems. Happily most of her own verses are unaffectedly childish: of her father she says 'Honest and well behaved is he And busy as a little Bee', and she did not fear once to proclaim she 'did not give a single damn'.

There are rare exceptions of precocity in this century: in the early twenties a book was published which had been written thirty years previously by a 9-year-old girl. This was Daisy Ashford's *Young Visiters*, a sort of juvenile Anita Loos, uproariously funny, which had a great success and has since been made into a musical. In the mid-fifties a little girl in France repeated much the same pattern of precocity, but this time the tone was more elevated and when 7-year-old Minou Drouet's poems were published there was a flurry of publicity and great amazement at so large a talent in so small a person. Four hundred years earlier she would have had many equals and rivals among the children of the Renaissance.

If in letters girls seem to equal boys there is no mention of them in music. Among infant prodigies Mozart must stand supreme: a composer at 4, playing in his embroidered coat before the courts of Vienna and Dresden when hardly older, at 6 performing in London having already made a tour of most of the European capitals, his achievement is unique, not only in the early flowering of his genius, but in its adult development. About two hundred years later another little boy, Yehudi Menuhin aged 5, set out on a world tour and is still delighting audiences with his violin.

On the whole children nowadays grow up later than ever before, and the modern parent's complaint about the teenager's precocity is merely a contemporary version of the eighteenth-century critic who protested against pert 11- and 12-year-old girls 'keeping select Companies with as much solemnity and expense as their Parents do with their own Acquaintance'. Today if there is not as much solemnity there is certainly more expense. But the prince of precocious children is without doubt Macaulay who as a small boy remarked to his mother when something had irritated her, 'Madam, it is part of that vast scheme of annoyance which governs this sub-lunary sphere'.

*Rembrandt
painted his son
Titus seriously
studying
his letters.*

Their books

Apart from moral treatises and school manuals there were no special
books for children before the seventeenth century when some of the
stories from current folk-lore began to be written down. The early
chapbooks hawked by pedlars, badly printed and illustrated by cheap
woodblocks, had among them 'Penny Sensationals', probably the
'fingle-fangles' so bitterly denounced by Bunyan, and some may
have amused but none were written for children. Their only stories
were *Aesop's Fables*, which Caxton printed in English, and *Tales from
the Gesta Romanorum*, a collection by an anonymous author, or
number of authors, drawn from many sources each complete with
its own 'moral', then considered as necessary as the story itself. In one
form or another, although the costumes changed, the religious
significance waned and the morals tended to disappear, these Tales
were in circulation from the fourteenth to the end of the eighteenth
century – a run any publisher might envy. The *Arabian Nights*, much

cut, early became available in most languages and by the fifteenth century there were also Malory's *Morte d'Arthur* and stories of the Knights of the Round Table, but these were rare and intended for the knights and their ladies, not for the young.

The first books written for a juvenile public were composed of hell-fire and tears. One of the earliest, James Janeway's *Token for Children* of 1671, gives an account of the 'exemplary lives and joyful deaths of several young children', such as the tale of Sarah aged 8 who was 'deeply sensible of the condition of her soul ... and wept bitterly to think what a case she was in'. The Puritans were vehement against the moral danger of light reading, they considered books a means of making children realize their sinful condition, and death-bed dramas as suitable reminders that 'they were not too little to go to hell' which 'is a terrible place ... worse than a thousand times whipping'. This horrible convention lingered on into nineteenth-century juvenile literature in which the young were frequently forced to contemplate the death agony and corpse of their playmate or parent. Little William of *East Lynne* was possibly the best-known example (though this was considered strong meat even at that time), Dickens's Paul Dombey and Little Nell, Eric in Dean Farrar's classic of *Little by Little*, and Mrs. Molesworth's Carrots were all calculated to draw tears from the miserable children. Oddly enough, since it was usually the good who died young, there was remarkably little moral incentive in such tales.

It is Perrault who first opened the doors of the fairy world which children still inhabit. The origins of many of his tales (the word folklore was not used until much later) are to be found in various forms in India, Persia or China: ogres owe their origin to the fear of Tartar hordes, from the 'Oigours' as Hungarians were then called; some authorities give Puss himself an Italian parentage long prior to Perrault, but he obstinately remains a courtier of the *Grand Siècle*. All the wonderful characters – the Sleeping Beauty, Little Red Riding Hood, Cinderella – wear and always will wear French seventeenth-century clothes, and inhabit a countryside dotted with French châteaux. Perrault, aged 69 and an Academician when he

Away with your playthings and down to your books: a governess gets a little boy ready for his lessons. Chardin.

published the Tales anonymously, later maintained they were told him by his old governess and called them *Les Contes de ma Mère l'Oye*, translated into English as *Tales from Mother Goose*. His subsequent *Cabinet des Fées* was not nearly as successful but it did contain one of the most wonderful stories in the world, *Beauty and the Beast*, which in this century was made by Jean Cocteau into a film of surpassing beauty.

Fairy tales became so popular that not only were they told to children but ladies and gentlemen read them out loud to each other in the Paris *salons*. This custom never spread across the Channel where adults were soon absorbed in two books which, although not written for children, were destined to become two of the great classics of juvenile literature: *Robinson Crusoe* and *Gulliver's Travels*. Andrew Selkirk's adventure on a desert island, as retold by Daniel Defoe, became the prototype of hundreds of stories in which some critics have observed the shadow of British colonialism complete with humble black, but children saw only a world of freedom where courage and initiative were required and rewarded, just as in *Gulliver's Travels* they ignored political satire and delighted in that contrast of scale and condition which is one of the prerequisites of the fairy world – Beauty and the Beast's ugliness, the discrepancy in size between Jack and the Giant, Tom Thumb and the spider. Alice, when she comes, will be both dwarf and giant.

This was a good beginning but none of these stories had been written specially for, but only adapted to children, whose books continued to be sternly didactic with great importance attached to morals. On this both the Church and the educationists were adamant: Oliver Goldsmith even proposed that in the interests of morality Dick Whittington should be deprived of his cat and only recognized as a model for industrious apprentices.

Even the first book which can be said to aim at amusement, the charming *Little Pretty Pocket Book* of 1744, was also intended to instruct. This was soon followed by John Newbery's Juvenile Library, which included the guileless Giles Gingerbread who loved books so much that he ate the words, and Tommy Tripp who rode all round London on his dog Jouleu asking how the children did, and if good, left an apple or an orange. At about the same date France produced *l'Ami des Enfants*, a 'small book for small hands' worthy of remembrance if for one sentence only in which the author asks 'how many long-toothed English have not THROWN themselves on their children'...

These same children would shortly become the concern of a redoubtable battalion of women: Hannah More restricted herself chiefly to educational matters, Mary Wollstonecraft tried to turn little girls into reasonable creatures and Maria Edgeworth became known as the novelist of the nursery, but all three were more interested in improvement-plus-knowledge than in pleasure.

The hell-fires of Puritan principles were only slowly extinguished and the 'awful warning' school continued into the nineteenth century. Ann and Jane Taylor put into neat verse a myriad moral precepts which are now forgotten, while their 'Twinkle, twinkle little Star' is still remembered affectionately. Mrs. Trimmer attempted the impossible task – and incurred Charles Lamb's wrath in so doing – of giving a semblance of morality to the *Arabian Nights*, while the *Instructor and Guide for Little Masters* and similar manuals included such extremes of adult wishful thinking as one boy saying to another 'How happy I am to have an elder brother who is so prudent', and the other replying 'I am no less happy that you are willing to be advised'. Though Struwwelpeter and his contemporaries were more concerned with the physical disasters which followed disobedience than with eternal damnation, morals were still paramount. Mrs. Sherwood considered no method too drastic to deal with original sin. In the *Fairchild Family* she describes how a father teaches his children the unwisdom of quarrelling by taking them at dusk through a gloomy wood and showing them the skeleton of a murderer hanging from a gibbet ... her *mèlange* of sadism and smugness may be revolting to modern ideas, but according to her time she was an intensely good woman – and children loved her books.

The real beginning of pure pleasure in children's books opened appropriately enough with a ball. The first gay and carefree story with no moral sting in its tail, no patronage and no pathos was *The Butterfly's Ball*, written by William Roscoe for his little son. The author, a serious historian, an M.P. and a well-known botanist, began:

'Come take up your hats, and away let us haste
To the Butterfly's Ball, and the Grasshopper's Feast.
The Trumpeter, Gadfly, has summon'd the Crew,
And the Revels are now only waiting for you.'

This is the authentic story-book voice, as telling today as when it was first heard in 1807, and continues the age-old tradition, kept alive by La Fontaine, that animals should speak in their right and proper characters: 'the Lion kingly, the Owl with pomp of phrase.'

In the same year Charles and Mary Lamb's *Tales from Shakespeare* appeared and were soon followed by Grimm's Tales and the stories of Hans Andersen. The brothers Grimm had collected tales handed down from generation to generation of peasants in Hesse and Cassel and these ancient legends were immediately successful, particularly in

71

Learning to read: 'The Lesson', by Chardin,
and RIGHT: *Gabrielle and Coco reading, by Renoir.*

England where they had the good luck to find the perfect illustrator in George Cruikshank. Hans Anderson's love of the inanimate object and his natural animism made great appeal to children, and his more mystical stories were almost equally popular in spite of their haunting sadness and the leit-motiv of death. The idea that myths could cloak unspeakable morals was still in the future: Cinderella, who dates back to early Egyptian times, had not yet been interpreted as a tale of human perversions dealing with foot fetishism and blood rites, but was simply a story in which the good win over the bad, and the poor become rich.

It is interesting to note that the great majority of fairy stories are of Celtic origin: although the first author credited with mentioning the fairies is a first-century Roman geographer, the Latin peoples, who spoil and pet their children in a way unknown to the Anglo-Saxons, have contributed least to their literature. The light of the Mediterranean is perhaps too clear for fantasy and it is from the northern mists that most of the little people have come.

Among the first books which told new tales for children, not old ones adapted, were the 'Peter Parley' books of early nineteenth-century America. The original 'Peter Parley', a pseudonym later used by a number of writers on both sides of the Atlantic, was horrified by such stories as Little Red Riding Hood, Jack the Giant Killer and Blue Beard, which he considered written 'for the express purpose of reconciling them [the children] to vice and crime'. Unreasonably enough when this honest man visited Europe in 1823 he was equally distressed to discover these tales were untrue.

By the middle of the nineteenth century it was realized that fairy tales were not only amusing but were significant signposts leading back to humanity's past. Mr. Ruskin himself, Slade Professor of Fine Art at Oxford, proclaimed that folk-lore was really important child-lore; he even wrote a fairy-story himself, and so refuted the Wife of Bath's complaint five centuries earlier, that clerics had banished the fairies. There was now no wall between fairyland and the nursery, which was becoming an important room in the house, just as the child was gaining in consequence. Andrew Lang began his great work of compiling the folk-tales of the world and the Green, Red, Blue and other colour Fairy Books became a treasure-trove for children of all countries.

The three daughters of Dean Liddell painted near Llandudno by Sir William Richmond. On the right kneels the little girl who was the Alice of Lewis Carroll's Wonderland.

Publishers began to realize that children were of many different kinds and special books began to be written for each particular section of the juvenile public, babies' books had jingles and clear pictures, boys' adventure tales were known as 'Robinsonnades' from the Swiss Family and Crusoe, and there were books suitable for girls. These last were a miserable few, and like the education of the girl through the ages, rarely predictable. Nevertheless any list which includes Charlotte M. Yonge's *Dove in the Eagle's Nest* and the *Daisy Chain* cannot be considered negligible, but there was little else for girls until L. T. Meade brought the new girls' schools into fiction at the end of the century.

The dawn of levity in children's books is usually traced to Miss Sinclair's *Holiday House* of 1839, though some credit should be given to Horace Walpole for composing five *Hieroglyphic Tales* for 5-year-old Anne Fitz-Patrick, which 'were undoubtedly written a little before the creation of the world and have ever since been preserved

74

by oral tradition in the mountains of Crampcraggiri, an uninhabited island not yet discovered', but it was Edward Lear's *Book of Nonsense* which finally released the delight of pure laughter.

Then Alice appeared.

Hitherto children had been moralized at or written for but they had never been pictured, now for the first time a special image of the child itself became familiar to the readers.

Among the many distinguished artists who illustrated children's books during the last forty years of the Victorian era three in particular influenced the whole world's vision of childhood: the first was Tenniel with Alice in the seventies, then in the eighties came Reginald Birch's Little Lord Fauntleroy and Kate Greenaway's children.

The small daughter of Dean Liddell for whom 'Alice' was written was not the model for the illustrations, for the original Alice was growing up while the Rev. Charles Dodgson, alias Lewis Carroll, was preparing the story for publication, and it is Mary Hilton Badcock's long golden hair which is held back by the familiar ribbon. To this day every child knows exactly how Alice looked, and thousands of little girls still have 'Alice' bands in their hair and call them so, and her dress with its 'pinny' continued to be routine wear for several decades after her appearance. All except her striped stockings. Few of these left the printed page and most of Alice's emulators politely ignored them. Such an absolute union between picture and story is hardly to be found again until Eloise came pelting down the corridors of the Plaza in 1957, with Ray Thompson's verse and Hilary Knight's drawings so complementary that one wonders which came first.

The Little Lord, who was a portrait of the author's second son, was the epitome of the 'top' in children's fashions and so great was his influence that generations of little boys were rendered miserable by their appalling garb of velvet suit and lace collar, though some, such as Romain Gary, seem to have enjoyed such trappings. Like Alice's striped stockings, Ceddie's scarlet ones were often omitted from the costume and a more conservative black substituted. It may come as a surprise to those who have not recently re-read this masterpiece that such expressions as 'I guess' and 'square' should appear in Mrs. Hodgson Burnett's sedate prose.

Mrs. Molesworth and Walter Crane were an equally happy author and artist alliance, and the latter's combination of seriousness and fantasy is the exact corollary of Mrs. Molesworth's comfortable upper-class houses in which tapestry rooms led through to fairyland and whose prim little inhabitants flew on the back of the cuckoo from the clock. Crane asserted that his own style was formed by two major experiences: some Japanese prints given him by a naval officer, and a tour of Italian Renaissance palaces. That such widely dissimilar influences should result in pictures of solid English children with blond curls and blooming cheeks seems hardly more surprising than that peacocks should talk.

Kate Greenaway's children are dressed in clothes of no ascertainable date but they had, and have, so vivid an appeal that 'Kate Greenaway' children still attend most English weddings and her name, not a king's or queen's, is used to describe the fashions she re-created from her memories of playing in the attic of a country house with the contents of an old chest.

As the nineteenth century drew to a close the list of distinguished authors who had written for children was truly impressive: to such famous names as Walter Scott, Dickens, Washington Irving, Gogol, Hawthorne, Pushkin and Oscar Wilde could be added Victor Hugo with his *L'Art d'être Grand-père*, while the great tradition of anthropomorphism was carried on by Kipling's *Jungle Books* and *Just So Stories* and that of adventure tales by Rider Haggard's *King Solomon's Mines*. Two great additions to juvenile literature now came from America, Fenimore Cooper's cowboys and Red Indians overran Europe, and Mark Twain's Huckleberry Finn became every boy's guide to freedom. In spite of these great names and successes a triumvirate of women with only small literary pretensions became and remain nursery best-sellers.

Mrs. Ewing will be always remembered for *The Brownies* who gave their name to Lord and Lady Baden-Powell's Girl Guides, though her *Daddy Darwin's Dovecot*, superbly illustrated by Randolph

Caldecott, is by far the better work, and Mrs. Nesbitt would be immortal if for no other reason than her genius in coining such names as the 'Would-be-goods' and the 'Ugly-wuglies'. Her children are as individual and real as the anecdote she recounts of her own youth when her brothers decided that she looked (in her best white frilly frock) so like a flower that they buried her in the garden. What a world away from the *beau monde* of the Comtesse de Ségur's *Petites Filles Modèles* with their beautiful boots, fine manners and elaborate fêtes, farther in thought, though not in time, than are the portraits of Winterhalter from those of Renoir.

The last of the triumvirate was Beatrix Potter who opened the new century with *Peter Rabbit*. From then until now her small books in which simple stories are perfectly balanced by exquisite illustrations have by-passed all barriers of class and climate, the manners and cosy homes of the Flopsy Bunnies and their friends in the fields and woods are known and loved by children of all races. Two years later Barrie's *Peter Pan* appeared and effortlessly took his place beside Alice, Puss, Snow-White and other immortal figures.

The ancient conception of anthropomorphism, brilliantly carried on by Belloc's *Bad Child's Book of Beasts* and later by de Brunhof's *Babar the Elephant*, has been taken over by the cinema, beginning with Felix the Cat, Minnie and Mickey Mouse, followed by *Bambi*, Walt Disney's inspired '*Fantasia*' and many others. Instead of a meagre few, millions of children's books are now printed each year but among them new fairy tales are rare. In a world which can be circumnavigated in fewer minutes than Jules Verne's hero took days, fairies are no longer considered first-class transport.

A perfect example of a good little girl reading her book: 'Beneath the lilies – tall, white garden lilies – The Princess slept, a charmed sleep alway; For ever were the fairy bluebells ringing, For ever thro' the night and thro' the day'.
Kate Greenaway.

Bowl away! bowl away!
Fast as you can;
He who can fastest bowl,
He is my man!
                    Kate Greenaway.

Their toys and games

Of the many aspects of a child's life through the centuries its toys and
games have changed least. The tiny carts, birds and animals found in
ancient tombs are remarkably similar to those in any modern toy-
shop and the street games of today repeat those of vanished cities. Toys
are the first instruments of a child's activity and games his first
attempt at co-operation: psychologists may look upon them as a
means of analysing behaviour, educationists as methods of teaching
and parents as a means of distraction, but all agree that the aim of
childish play is the discharge of superfluous energy.

The old English word for toy throws light on its intention, 'teon'
meant pull-toy and action is the very essence of play: spinning tops,
bouncing balls, rolling marbles and pulling carts have amused
children through thousands of years and at the same time taught them
the first principles of movement and sound.

The child's earliest toy, one which both moves and makes a noise,

78

In the sixteenth-century streets the boys bowled hoops, played at hobby-
horses, pig-a-back and leap-frog just as they do today. Bruegel.   79

is usually the rattle, whose invention is ascribed to Archytas of Tarentum. Even such serious philosophers as Pliny and Paracelsus recommended its use particularly when made of coral, whose colour was believed to vary with the health of the wearer and was considered efficacious against evil spirits. The babies of Southern Europe still wear amulets of it to ward off the Evil Eye and until recently every new baby's layette contained a coral rattle, though early examples were more often circles or horse-shoes of metal whose transverse bars were threaded with tinkling discs.

The ball shares with the doll (which will have a chapter to itself) the highest antiquity among toys and both have been found among the earliest known human remains. The ancient Egyptians made balls from papyrus or plaited reeds or of leather filled with husks of grain similar to those of stuffed deer-skin still used by the Red Indians, the Japanese made them of tightly pressed tissue paper bound with fancy string, and woollen balls were known to the Romans at least three centuries before Christ. The first bouncing ball was probably made from the inflated bladder of a sheep or goat, rather like our present

'Rattles, timbrels, toys Take little infants with their noise.'
Marie-Zephyrine, the infant daughter of Louis XV. Nattier.

David Allan painted Lord and Lady Cathcart and their family in the grounds of their house engaged in the first cricket match ever played in Scotland.

football, and the bouncing ball of beautifully woven split cane continues to be made in Malaya. An early Egyptian fresco shows an elaborate ball-catching game in which some of the players have to keep their arms crossed, and the Greeks were known to play a ball-game with rigid rules laid down for the distances between the antagonists.

Solid balls of wood, composition or rubbed marble to roll along the ground have been used for centuries for bowls or skittles, which were probably developed from the ancient pagan rite of 'rolling the sphere'. A mystical significance has always been attached to the rolling of a stone from one place to another and it was believed that the dead played Tali, or knucklebones, with each other. Cricket has a Celtic ancestor in the game of 'Stonies'; football, that game of 'beastly furie and extreme violence', still remains popular; and in Japan a similar sport was believed to be played by strange spirits with the bodies of monkeys and the faces of children, which tallies with the Irish and Scotish belief that the ball-game of Hurley is a favourite pastime of fairies.

Tennis, once described as the game 'least repugnant to moralists' and already popular in Chaucer's time, was developed from the *jeu de paume* in which the ball was driven from the palm of the hand covered by a glove or by cords wound round it to accelerate the speed of the ball, similar to the cane scoop used in pelota today. Both tennis and golf were taught to children at a much earlier age than they are today.

A relative newcomer among ball-toys is the balloon, that lovely multi-coloured light-as-air ball which before the last War was sold by a fat lady at Hyde Park Gate whose ascent to heaven (and once she let go of her basket her bevy of balloons would inevitably uplift her) was so fearfully desired by the little boy who did not WANT such a thing to happen, but did HOPE he would be present if it did. Recently a balloon became a cinema star, and the adventures of *The Red Balloon* from the time when it escaped from the hands of its young owner until it was recaptured, forms one of the loveliest films for children ever contrived.

The top goes back to the beginning of history. It is thought to have originated in Japan where top-spinning became elevated to a mathematical science and was as important as kite-flying in China and Malaya. All over the East literally hundreds of different types of top-play were known and practised as much by adults as by children. In Europe there are references in Virgil to boys playing with whip-tops, but those started by means of a string wound round a weighted tip were probably brought to Europe from the Far East by Dutch seamen and did not come into general use until the middle of the sixteenth century. In some districts at festival time large whip-tops were put at the disposal of the peasants by their local lord and an eye-witness writes that 'to walk down the village road in top-time was as difficult as to walk on ice – tops flew under one's feet, whips curled

Children learnt grown-up games far earlier than they do now: a small   83
Dutch boy beginning to play golf regardless of his long skirts
and inappropriate hat. Pietr de Hooch.

around the ankles, and little boys looked baleful when somebody touched a large spinning top and made it die. Drivers kept a watchful eye, for the tops dashed out like wild things under the horses' hooves and boys ran after them'. The top in Europe never had the importance it had in the East and only half a dozen kinds became popular, of which the favourite is the string-driven top once known as the Flying Propeller but recently renamed by schoolboys the Flying Saucer. Rarities are the whistling top with a paper lantern in its head, the large top which releases smaller tops from its girth as it spins, and the new Swedish gyroscope made in plastic and known as the Tippy Tap, which will turn upside down and spin on its head.

Most toys were sold through the pedlars who hawked the small necessities of life from village to village and the special toy-shop, which had its apotheosis in the ballet of *Boutique Fantasque* with Derain's exquisite settings and costumes, was a nineteenth-century development, though in seventeenth-century Paris the 'Noah's Ark' was already famous. Some toy-shops, such as 'le Nain Bleu' in Paris and Hamleys in London have become internationally known and the family of Lines, who have held a Royal Warrant for over a hundred years, still make dolls' perambulators as beautifully sprung and padded as those used by their young owners, though none as luxurious as that made for the Sultan of Zanzibar's children fifty years ago, upholstered in white kid and completed by silver fittings but, alas, the fascinating shop in Holborn which used to purvey magical deceptions has vanished, and the Lowther Arcade off the Strand, famous for its toy-shops in the sixties, is no more. Nowadays the individual shop devoted solely to toys is again becoming rare and toys are sold at the chemists, the stationers or general stores. But there are exceptions.

When H. G. Wells wrote a book on children's games in 1913 he complained of the finicky and vulgar toys then available and accused the toy-shops of 'trifling with great possibilities': some time later this came to the notice of a young Quaker school-teacher and his wife and in due course the famous Paul and Marjorie Abbatt partnership was formed. This was at a time when the Nursery School Association was proving that play could be as educational as lessons, and the

Abbatts' shop with its lovely hand-made toys became the Mecca of child, parent and teacher alike. Thirty years later an enlightened enthusiast tracked down and acquired the last remaining Pollock toy theatres, together with some of the original designs 'Penny Plain and Twopence Coloured' of scenery and costume which the little shop in Hoxton, destroyed by the war, had made and sold to all theatre amateurs as well as to children. Now a special shop for toy-theatres has been opened near Covent Garden and children can once again obtain their own private theatres as well as all the plays and puppet-actors they require.

Puppet theatres have been known from remote times in many parts of the world but nowhere have had as much importance as in the Far East where some Japanese great families still count among their retainers a stage-manager of puppet-shows, just as Spanish and Italian nobles did in the past. The puppet-shows of Malaya and Java are repositories of their folk-lore. Sir Stamford Raffles acknowledged he learned much of the people's history from their shadow-plays which recount the old legends of the East just as the puppet-shows of Sicily continue to re-enact the rescue of Clorinda by Tancred and the victory of Christian heroes over the infidels. Not a child in the island who does not know the entire story (whose cycle takes a whole year to tell) of the paladins and their prowess.

The possibility of throwing figures on the screen by means of lanterns was first demonstrated in Europe in the thirteenth century by Roger Bacon, who was promptly accused of black magic, but managed to persuade the Pope not only to pronounce his invention harmless but to play with it. In the eighteenth century it began to be used for educational purposes though Grimm considered it best for childish entertainments, and the wonderful lantern continued to show children enchantments and marvels until the arrival of the cinema. Nothing can efface from the memories of those old enough to have experienced it the peculiar smell of the magical apparatus and the thrilling moment when the lights were turned down and flickering pictures appeared on the white sheet.

Mechanical toys also date from remote antiquity. Egyptian

children had enchanting crocodiles and hippos with snapping jaws, several of which have survived, Aristotle ascribes the movement of a certain famous Venus to a quantity of quick-silver placed in the body, Herodotus writes of a fête given for Osiris when mysterious means were used to give the semblance of life to the god's figure, and the great statue of Jupiter Ammon was known to move its head. Archytas, author of the rattle, is also credited with inventing the first flying bird, such as the wooden dove Hadrian speaks of which flew by having its body filled with air, and the first singing bird was Hero of Alexandria's bird-whistle of nearly two centuries before Christ. This tiny earthenware bird contained a tube ending in a little whistle which, when water was poured into the funnel and the air driven out, made a bubbling noise like a bird's song. It is still made in the same way and found all over the world. The mechanical birds invented to amuse poor Charles v flew about so naturally that the Superior of the Convent was alarmed lest magic was employed, but the sad Emperor, with half Europe and a good part of the East and the Americas to play with, had to be distracted from the tedium of his existence by mechanical figures, and passed his time with toy soldiers who beat drums and blew trumpets.

Animated figures were much used in the Middle Ages to impress the ignorant laity and puppets have always been associated with witchcraft. In some of these early figures streams of sand were used to displace the limbs, but later this method was superseded by mercury and by the magnetized needle. One of the most famous was the speaking head made in the thirteenth century by Albert le Grand, Bishop of Ratisbon, which took him thirty years to perfect and one of his disciples, fearing black magic, less than thirty minutes to destroy.

By the eighteenth century the fashion for automata had become a mania and extraordinarily complicated and ingenious examples were constructed that were more suited to grown-ups than to children.

> 'An ivory box the right hand holds
> From which by curious springs,
> A little bird of finely wrought gold
> Comes forth and sweetly sings.'

*The pull-toy of to-day
is more often an engine than
a cart and horse. His son
Valentine by Henry Lamb.*

But the inventive designer Vaucanson went one better and constructed a duck which quacked, swam, ate and even evacuated – a sad waste of what must have been unusual technical skill. These mechanical toys always had a strong appeal to Oriental people and many of gold or silver, some elaboratedly jewelled, have found their way from Paris or Birmingham to the treasure rooms of Rajahs for the amusement of idle adults as well as the curious young.

Amongst the oldest known moving toys in the world is that of the chickens which, by the use of a lead counter-balance, endlessly pick up grains of corn and which is still hand-carved in Russia today.

The toy carts found in Egyptian tombs have changed not at all through the centuries and those found in Egyptian tombs closely resemble the ones in modern toy-shops, and those to which Greek children harnessed mice had axle pins similar to still extant sixteenth-century models from Nuremburg. Sometimes toy carts were made

Pulling carts is fun in any age: the children of Mr. and Mrs. H. J. S. Pietrzak, by Mary Potter, 1955. BELOW: *A detail from the painting by George Stubbs of Josiah Wedgwood and his family at Etruria Hall.*

A splendid development of the hobby-horse was the mechanical horse on which Jean Monet proudly bicycled in 1872. Claude Monet.

large enough for the child to ride in, such as the one listed among the gifts to Charles VI when a child in the 1380's, to which he harnessed dogs for steeds, but by the time Monet painted his little son the wheel and chain had been invented and instead of dogs to pull him the little boy is seen proudly pedalling about the garden on a 'mechanical horse'.

The earliest form of playing horses was the hobby-horse on a stick which was known in ancient China and makes a frequent appearance in European paintings, but is now rarely seen when little boys prefer to sit and pedal a miniature motor car rather than run with an imaginary horse. Two contrasting stories of hobby-horse games are told of the King of Sparta and the King of Spain ... when Aegilias of Sparta was taken unawares playing hobby-horses with his children he begged his friend not to mention so undignified a pastime but when, rather more than a thousand years later, Henry IV was caught by the Dutch Ambassador on all fours with his small son on his back,

The sons of Daniel Seton, Governor of the East India Company at Surat Castle,
by an unknown artist. One is shown proudly aloft on his rocking horse,
the other attended by a native servant.

he only paused long enough to ask if the Ambassador were a father.
On hearing that he was, the king replied that in that case he would
make another turn.

The early rocking horse was a primitive affair which showed only
a head fixed to a clumsy half-circle of wood, but by the eighteenth
century the whole animal was elaborately carved, either painted or
covered with cowhide, and had legs attached to shaped rockers. Late
in the last century swing-irons replaced the capsizable rocker and
although the mount was still referred to as a rocking horse, strictly
speaking it was one no longer. In spite of their waning popularity
there is in London a firm which still employs elderly men to carve
rocking horses by hand, in the same way in which they have been
made for generations.

In the past each season had its appropriate toys and games: during
Holy Week children were given tiny copes, censers, monstrances and

pyxes to play with, hoops were not bowled before Christmas, tops
followed later, grottoes were special to St. James's Day, skipping
began on Good Friday, marbles were not put out until April or May,
handball was played in Yorkshire at Easter, for the prize of a tansy
cake. Until well into the nineteenth century two Gingerbread Fairs
were held each year in Birmingham and none of the cake was
available at any other period. This sensible arrangement, which
ensured that the child played with a toy or a game for only a short
time and then had something new to distract him, began to lose
ground as religious festivals were discontinued and now most toys,
like our foodstuffs, are available all the year round and the particular
flavour and variety of the seasons are lost. Only the figurines of the
Christmas legend continue to be special to the season, and each
December beautiful little crêches re-tell in miniature the story of the
Holy Birth.

Most children's games can be classified into those which develop
individual skill, those which demand mutual co-operation and those
which imitate the occupations of grown-ups. European children play
at doctors or weddings, small Australian aborigines at 'carrying off
brides', Eskimo children build snow huts. In Mexico little boys were

*Aping their elders in the nineteenth century: a group of children playing
at doctors, by F. D. Hardy.*

No little girl could be more adorably feminine than this shuttlecock player, with her frilled cap and her huswife hung by a ribbon from her waist. Chardin.

provided at birth with models of their father's weapons or tools, at three the Mongol boy was given a bow of suitable size and as his strength increased so did the size of the bow, just as Western boys are given small, and later larger, weapons of destruction. Many boys' games are associated with trials of strength (Tug of War), with taking prisoners and territories, (I'm the King of the Castle), or with pursuit, of which 'Fox and Geese' is one of the oldest known examples and an excellent illustration of it can be seen carved on the cloister benches of Gloucester Cathedral. The distinction between the sexes, though less marked than it was, still exists, and if little girls play at Cowboys and

Indians no boy would be seen with a doll. In Japan the battledore and shuttlecock (which should be 'cork' in reference to its composition) was associated solely with girls, and it was customary to send them to a house where a daughter had been born, while boys were presented with a bow and arrow. The rivalry between the two sexes is still summed up by the question of 'What are little boys made of?' and the

A small boy of 5 has placed his feathered hat on a stool
but is prepared to play at battledore in spite of
his cumbersome full skirt and a huge stiffened collar.
English School, circa 1616.

contemptuous answer, 'Slugs and snails and puppy dogs' tails That's what little boys are made of', and the smug 'Sugar 'n Spice 'n all that's nice' in reply to a similar query about the origin of little girls.

Today both sexes bowl hoops with equal zest if and when traffic congestion permits, but in the many fifteenth- and sixteenth-century street scenes of this sport boys only are to be seen bowling their hoops

Children still bowl hoops in the streets and dogs bark at them, but only clowns

in the road. The wooden hoop, known to both Greeks and Romans, was superseded by the Victorian iron controlled by a 'skimmer' (a handle with a hook at one end), but these soon became the sign of a street urchin while a 'lady's child' used hand-made hoops of un-seasoned wood steamed into shape. Since 1939 these have been diffi-cult to obtain and the modern hoop is of laminated beech veneer which forms a perfect circle without pins or joins.

Among games which enshrine long-forgotten superstitions or

customs is 'Nuts in May' (it should be 'knots'), which refers to the folk-custom of marriage by capture and is somewhat similar to the Greek Flower Games played in circles or lines with singing questions and answers. 'Here we go round the Mulberry Bush' is a descendant of a fertility rite, 'London Bridge is broken Down' is thought to refer to blood-sacrifices offered at the time of its foundation,

in the circus nowadays walk on stilts. Douce Prints.

and 'Ring-a-ring of Roses' recalls the superstition that a sneeze casts out a demon who must be exorcized immediately by exclaiming 'God bless you'.

Blindman's Buff has a long history, so has Hop-scotch or Tip-cat which was played by native children in India, who introduced it to the Portuguese through whom it came to Europe. The street game of 'odd squares' is related to pachisi, played at the court of Akbar on a floor inlaid with marble squares with slaves dressed in different

After a country walk in high laced boots, Mary Wyndham returns with her lap full of flowers. Val Prinsep.

*Diversions for a wet day have changed
not at all through the years. 'Card Houses' in the late eighteenth
century, by Chardin.* BELOW: *'The Master Builder', a portrait
of his son Esmond painted by Antony Devas in the 1950's.*

colours to represent the pieces. Suetonius describes the Emperor Augustus playing a somewhat similar game with young lads in his palace, and in Italy the main square of Montefeltre is composed of black and white squares on which, once a year, a game is still played by men on horse-back as the pieces, each rider attired in splendid Renaissance costume.

Marbles is a comparatively modern title for an ancient game formerly played with the stones of cherries or with chestnuts or cobs, and derives its present name from the substance of such bowls as Drake was playing with when the Armada hove in sight. The veined glass marbles which are now collectors' pieces were not introduced until the sixties of the last century. The popular game of 'stonies', which consists of dropping a metal disc or stone straight on to an agreed target, came to England through the Roman legionaries who used water-worn pebbles as ammunition. Its name was modernized during the last war into 'bombers', for the play of London street urchins keeps amazingly up-to-date and inevitably reflects their epoch: during the second decade of this century two games were re-christened 'Harem Skirt' and 'I can do the Tango' after two songs then popular. Norman Douglas asserted that no less than a thousand different games were played in the London streets before World War I but he may have counted somewhat recklessly, certainly there are far fewer today when street play-space has shrunk but more and more playgrounds have been provided which tend to encourage organized, rather than individual games.

Indoor games have also greatly diminished in numbers and popularity and few families now forgather to play various card and table games. The equipment of any Edwardian family when preparing for their annual exodus to the seaside always contained such distractions for a wet day as a pack of 'Happy Families' and other cards, a box of tiddlywinks, one of dominoes and a board of draughts, and children learnt to play lotto, chess and piquet far more, and at an earlier age, than they do now when there is a cinema round the corner and a television set at home. On the other hand beach-games were rarer and there were a series of bathing taboos which decreed

Looking longingly out of the window, Rembrandt's plump little girl rests her elbows on the sill. Perhaps she is thinking 'Maytime is to the meadows coming in, And cowslips peeps have gotten eer so big, And water blobs and all their golden kin Crowd round the shallows by the striding brig'.

it was not safe to paddle for the first two days, or to bathe more than once a day and then always in the morning. One had to be ducked immediately on entering the sea and carefully guarded against the sun. As for undressing on the beach or sun-bathing, these were unheard of diversions.

The many songs and games which have death as their theme prove plainly that to children the thought of this experience is no more fearful than any other unknown event: they are curious but not apprehensive. One small girl of 4 remarked to her mother 'I haven't died yet' in much the same way as she might refer to any other activity in which she had not yet participated, and was not at all dismayed at being told she could do it only once: 'for ever' being a state no child, and few adults, can comprehend.

Horror stories have always been popular with children and London urchins sing (or did until the Welfare State came into being),

> 'I am a little beggar-girl
> My mother she is dead,
> My father is a drunkard
> And would give me no bread
> Bless my poor mother –
> Her coffin shall be black
> Six angels at her back –
> Two to watch and two to pray,
> And two to carry her soul away.'

At the sea-side even to wet the toes was a great adventure in 1853. 'Ramsgate Sands', by Frith; but RIGHT: *by 1879 Renoir's 'Petite Pêcheuse' was sensibly dressed for shrimping.*

There is no doubt that a cathartic delight is experienced in singing about death and burial, and the death of 'Cock Robin' has always been a favourite with street children who arm themselves for the fray with saucepan lids in lieu of shield. An ancient song from the Champagne district, but curiously enough called *'le pont de Londres'*, tells the tale of a disobedient girl who insisted on going to a ball in her white dress against her mother's wishes and met with a fatal accident: the song ends with relish on these moral lines

'Votre fille Aline est morte et enterrée
Voila le sort des enfants obstinés!'

Some games reflect the child's own wishes: many bruises and bumps have been sustained by those who want to fly like Peter Pan, and the custom of African savages beating their fetish images to rouse them to action has its counterpart in the young whipping their dolls or toy animals in order to make them respond. The habit of breaking their toys to find out what is inside is universal but few parents' composure would be the equal of Charles Fox's, who, when his younger son positively craved to smash a watch, gave him one and allowed him to break it; and when the child had been promised he could watch a wall being blown up with gunpowder, but missed the event, the father had the wall rebuilt and blown up again, merely remarking that one should never break promises to children. This is experiment on a scale rarely enjoyed by the young, though privileged adults sheltering under the umbrella of 'scientific research' would think nothing of such trifles.

The little jockey of Artemision was not seen by human eyes for over 2,000 years. In 1928 a sunken ship off the coast of Attica was discovered which contained a shipment of statues, probably loot, among them this lively figure of a small boy intent on winning the race. It is thought to date from the third century B.C.

*A little boy well-pleased
with his strange pet;
'Boy with marzocco',
fifteenth century
Florentine
verde di Prato figure.*

Their pets

A child's first friend is usually a pet; a friend who does much to develop the instincts of protectiveness and chivalry, and who evokes respect for a different kind of person. A pet is very actually a person to a child, for anthropomorphism is as natural to the first years of childhood as to the early ages of man and makes little distinction between two feet and four. When one little girl, an amateur of Beatrix Potter, caught sight of her first squirrel seated on a bough cracking a nut, after a first glance of delighted recognition her eyes filled with tears – for she realized that as Timothy Tiptoes was out minus his red coat his mother would scold him. Many adults do not quite outgrow anthropomorphism in regard to their own particular pets; nor are they surprised if the inhabitants of the Zoological Gardens remind them irresistably of several close friends.

The pets cherished by children today are much the same as those which have been known and loved since the beginning of history –

Two aspects of the cat: LEFT: *Julie Manet's purrs cosily in her arms. Renoir. The cat of Jenny and Laura Donington, twin step-daughters of Sir Andrew Cohen, looks out with a keenly predatory air. E. Box.*

the familiar cat and dog, age-long rivals yet perennial companions who, like humans, have rarely found a way of living together in peace and amity. Cats were popular house pets in the time of the Pharaohs when they went by the names of MAAU or CHAOU, and their mummified bodies have been found buried in the same tombs as their small owners, so that the loved pet could accompany the child on its journey to the Kingdom of the Dead. The mysterious qualities of the cat were early recognized: it was revered as a god in ancient

*Puss at its pussiest:
a cat as intrigued by the
dead mouse as the small
boy is frightened. Boilly.*

*Don Manuel Osario de
Zuniga's two cats have
their eyes fixed only too
firmly on his pet bird.
Goya.*

Egypt and has appeared at various times in the guise of a magician or as the familiar of witches. Perhaps it was this association with black magic which led to the horrible ceremony of St. John's festival when a basket or sack of live cats was thrown on to a bonfire and the people afterwards carried away the ashes, which were considered to be lucky. Louis XIII as a child interceded with his parents for the wretched animals but was only temporarily successful, and that horrid young man Louis XIV, wreathed in roses, himself lit the bonfire and danced around it.

The cat's cunning is as proverbial as the dog's constancy, but while there are no examples of dogs as unscrupulously wily as the booted Puss who raised his master to the Marquisate of Carabas, many cats have been known to be as faithful, if not as percipient, as Dick Whittington's companion. Their independence of character is also widely acclaimed, indeed 'The Cat who walked by Himself' was by no means unique. Yet most children consider pussy as cosy and cushionable, and the dog, in a dashing more agreeable way, as more dominating. They know that dogs are simply not allowed the usual freedom of cats to rove at night, which one little boy accounted for as a reward to cats for voluntarily washing their faces. It is true that dogs are more interested in human activities and have a stronger wish to control us, but some cats are affectionate to the point of clingingness and less affectionate cats can also be very demanding; the unscrupulousness of faithful Puss in Boots is the real clue to their independence. Most domestic dogs have a conscience and cats, however warm-hearted and courteous, have not. It is well understood in nurseries that, of the two endearing self-willed creatures, the dog knows when he has done wrong but parallels this with a great sense of his rights, while the cat has no sense of right and wrong whatever. The distinctive characteristics of cat and dog are summed up in Christina Rossetti's jingle

> 'Kitty has such pretty ways;
> Doggie scampers when I call,
> And has a heart to love us all.'

The Eastern aristocrats of the feline world, the Siamese and Persian cats, are rarely nursery folk, the former usually too nervous and high strung, the latter too reserved and disdainful for childish play. Whereas some people might be surprised that the two white Persian cats on the other side of the Tapestry Room could talk, no one would wonder at them sitting on white satin cushions. The popular nursery cat is usually a tabby of unknown extraction or a marmalade, such as the 'Orlando' immortalized by Katherine Hale.

One of the most remarkable characteristics of the cat is its unchanging appearance: many cats of ancient Egypt are indistinguishable from the pussies of today, but dogs have varied as much as dress. At different epochs children have cherished such contrasting types as the tiny Maltese terrier, the small spaniel, the vast St. Bernard of Victorian lithographs, the Great Dane who succumbed to little Lord Fauntleroy's charm, the collie of Edwardian pictures, and the sturdy corgis made popular by the present Royal family.

Very small or very large, dogs are equally loved. RIGHT: *A little girl in a yellow and white dress clasps her tiny terrier who wears a bell on a scarlet ribbon. Dutch School.* BELOW: *One of the Dashwood children tries in vain to put her arms round a huge mastiff. Sir William Beechey.*

The Egyptians worshipped the dog under the onomatopoeic name of 'Oupouaout'; the ancients feared him under that of Cerberus; he is immortalized as the dog-star Sirius, associated with the source of life as it rose as the time of the Nile floods; and mummies and effigies of dogs have been found in early tombs in such diverse countries as China, Egypt and Mexico. A fine Egyptian example in carved ivory has movable limbs, and another, now in the Louvre, shows a magnificent wolf-dog with a bell hung on a rope round its neck, while in China beautifully modelled terra-cotta figures were put in tombs to accompany their masters on the road to Heaven, for the dogs' capacity of finding its way was a well-known trait. The Aztecs believed everyone should have a red-haired dog buried with him to show him the road to the gods, and the people of the frozen north explained the shimmering light of the aurora as a reflection of ghostly dog-teams carrying the departed spirits to heaven. Although not usually credited with such magical powers as the cat, dogs are often believed to have the power of speech – in Africa it was generally thought all dogs could talk – and some accounts say it was Tobias' dog which announced the return of his son.

Somewhat pessimistically addressed by George Crabbe as 'the only creature faithful to the end', the dog's characteristic of loyalty was early recognized: the god Anubis in the shape of a dog guarded the dead Osiris, just as Abel's body was saved from wild beasts by the dogs which kept the flock.

The dog does not figure as prominently as the cat in Greek art but that it was often much loved is proved by an ancient epitaph which says 'Thou who passest on the path, if haply thou dost mark this monument, laugh not, I pray thee, though it is a dog's grave; tears fell for me, and the dust was heaped above me by a master's hand, who likewise engraved these words on my tomb'. Its faithfulness is a constant theme of poetry, Virgil sang its fidelity, Homer remarks the constancy of Ulysses' dog, and Alexander rewarded his dog Paritas, who died during the campaign in India, by naming a city after him.

The best-known example in Western literature of the dog's high quality is the story of Gelert, the favourite hound of Llewellyn. One day when this Welsh Prince returned from hunting he found the dog covered with blood and his baby's cradle empty. Wild with fury he stabbed the poor beast whose death-howl awakened the child who, unharmed, lay beside a slaughtered wolf of enormous size which the faithful hound had fought and killed to save the baby's life. A similar story is recounted of Tsar Piras of Russia and examples of other loyal and courageous beasts abound in ancient tales. The *Gesta Romanorum* recounts the legend of the knight Follicus in which the predatory animal is a snake, as it is in the Sanskrit version where the rôle of the brave dog is taken by an ichneumon; in the Arabian it is a weasel, in the Mongolian a pole-cat and in the Hitopadesa an otter. These legendary figures have a near-contemporary in *Jack of the Bushveld*, and heroic animals abound in the cinema: *Rescued by Rover* was an immensely popular film in 1905 which showed a dog rescuing a baby from kidnappers, and the exploits of Rin Tin Tin in the twenties are not yet forgotten. Alas, that the sad little Dauphin's pet dog Coco, who was allowed to accompany him to his prison in the Temple, had neither the brute strength nor the magical powers to help his poor young master.

Most of the dogs recorded in early history were hunting dogs which are found among the earliest known graphic illustrations. They appear frequently in Egyptian and Assyrian bas-reliefs and in medieval tapestries and manuscripts, and later were conspicuous in many of the canvases of Veronese, Van Dyck and many other painters.

Well-trained animals were often offered as presents between royalties and there are many references to such gifts from Tudor and Stuart sovereigns to European potentates, in return for which the English monarchs received outlandish wolf-hounds and poodles. The latter originally came from Russia but was bred extensively in Germany, where it got its name from 'pudelin', i.e. to splash, as it was originally used as a water-dog for its specially greasy hair easily repelled water. The Pomeranian, which also came from Central Europe at a relatively early date, did not become popular until Queen Victoria made it fashionable.

It is thought possible that the dogs known to have been offered to

Master James Paine was painted with a Pomeranian and little else at a time when the childish nude and these dogs were two new fashions. George Romney.

the Chinese Emperor Kou-Tzu in the early seventh century may have been Maltese terriers which had made the long journey from Constantinople across Asia by the Silk Road. Though rare today the Maltese is one of the oldest known breeds in the world: a statuette of one was found in a tomb of the time of Rameses II, Strabo speaks well of them, calling them Canis Melitei, from the town of Melita or Malta, and says that though they were so small yet they were not small in courage and lovingness. This appealing little dog gambols into dozens of Renaissance portraits, its tiny form and white curls a perfect foil to the grandiose velvets and dignified bearing of its owners, or sits, a jewelled collar round its neck, on a cushion at the feet of la Dame à la Licorne.

The first monarch in England to cherish dogs solely as pets was Charles II, whose love of his toy spaniels was so excessive that he took them to bed with him as richly dressed as himself, and Pepys complained bitterly of the King playing with them when he should have been attending to matters of state, but he did not go so far as Louis

XI who had a gold collar set with rubies for his pet dog 'Cherami'. The spaniel is said to have came originally from Hispaniola, now called Haiti, but was bred at the courts of Europe, particularly in Spain, though its first appearance in paint is thought to be a white and reddish toy spaniel in a picture by Titian dated 1505. The breed was brought to England by Charles I who gave his name to the small black and tan variety, bred on one side from a Japanese spaniel probably brought by the Dutch from the Far East, kept jealously by the Duke of Norfolk at Arundel, to which no one else was given access. (Japanese spaniels were not officially imported into England until the 1860's.) The Cavalier breed is very near the original type and not unlike the Kooikerhond the Flemish painters loved to introduce into their pictures. When the English court was at Greenwich the many Royal dogs were kept on an island just opposite the Palace which still bears their name – the Isle of Dogs – and were so pampered that they were even allowed in churches where special 'dog-whippers' were detailed to keep them in order.

The three Gaddi children who look full of barely controlled mischief, and their toy dog, by Sophonisba Anguisciola.

*Peter Gimpel and his
shadowy dog,
by Marie Laurencin.*

Most spaniels are good companions for children and rarely turn on
them: one had good cause to, but didn't. Lord Berners recounts that
as a little boy of 6 he heard grown-ups remarking on a dog's capacity
to swim when thrown in water: wondering if a similar phenomenon
would occur should a dog be thrown into the air – would it fly? – he
heaved his mother's heavy spaniel up to the window ledge and gave
it a push. Far from flying the dog fell – unhurt – into a lilac bush
beneath the window. Most unfairly, as he thought, the little boy was
substantially punished by his parents, but the dog bore him no ill-will.

Another imported pet which was an immediate success in England
was the pug, known on the Continent as Mops. Originally a Temple
dog in China, it was brought to Europe by East Indiamen in the
eighteenth century and so quickly became a favourite that when Mrs.
Thrale went to Italy in 1786 she remarked on the number she saw
there, for she considered them already out of fashion at home.
Obviously they became even more popular, if less fashionable, for
they seem to have been an indispensable adjunct to Victorian in-

teriors and their flat little faces and pudgy bodies appear on innumerable pictures, embroidered cushions and china ornaments of that period. The pug's amiable disposition is probably due to its thousands of years in the service of the Son of Heaven and it is particularly forbearing with children. In her memoirs Lady Diana Cooper recalls that it was the only dog allowed in the nursery as it was never known to retaliate ill-advised tugs or slaps. It inspired one of the most heartfelt poems of praise ever dedicated to any animal:

'O lovely O most charming Pug
They graceful air and heavenly mug
The beauties of his mind do shine
And every bit is shaped so fine
Your very tail is most devine
Your teeth is whiter than the snow
You are a great buck and a bow
Your eyes are of so fine a shape
More like a Christians than an ape
His cheeks is like the roses blume
Your hair is like the ravens plume
His noses cast is of the roman
He is a very pretty woman
I could not get a rhyme for roman
So was obliged to call it weoman.'   *Margery Fleming*

An even greater success than the pug, but less partial to children, was the 'peke' whose origin is as romantic as any story-teller could wish. At the time of the Boxer rebellion in 1860 Lord John Hay was sent in command of a naval detachment to relieve the British Residency in Pekin. When he was going through the apartments of the Emperor's aunt in the Summer Palace, in a corner of a room behind a curtain, he found five tiny puppies and being an Englishman, in the middle of an extremely dangerous military operation several hundreds of miles from his base and several thousands from home, he carefully picked up the puppies and managed to bring them all back to England. He gave one of the curious little beasts – by now they looked like no other dog seen before – to Queen Victoria and another to his sister, the Duchess of Richmond, who bred the famous litter from which the first pekes in England were descended. Queen Victoria's, called by the unattractive name of 'Loopy', became a great favourite, 'pekes' became the fashion and by the end of the century it was thought that 'anyone who was anyone' had one.

In its previous existence in China the pekingese was the pet of the Chinese Imperial house throughout seven dynasties (though the term 'pekingese' only dates from the seventeenth century), and there are hundreds of portraits of these tiny creatures on the scrolls known collectively as the *Imperial Dog Book*. The puppies were said to be suckled by the Imperial concubines, a custom also occasionally followed in Europe where high-born lap-dog puppies were sometimes sent out to human foster-mothers. One Italian woman who later saw one of her foster-puppies killed in an accident, had hysterics, and said it was like losing a child of her own.

Strict pronouncements governed the pekes' appearance. Among the 'Pearls dropped from the lips of her Imperial Majesty Tsi-Hai, Dowager Empress of the Flowery Land' was the following description of the ideal pekingese: 'Let the Lion-dog be small ... let its face be black ... and for its colour, let it be that of the lion, a golden sable, to be carried in the sleeve of a yellow robe ... let it comport itself with dignity ... let it bite the foreign devils instantly ... let it be dainty in its food that it shall be known for an Imperial Dog by its fastidiousness ... let it be lively that it may afford entertainment by its gambols.' It has continued to do so in England for a hundred years and its popularity has never waned – nor has its independence of character softened.

A dog indisputably associated with England is the bulldog which has been specially bred for bull-baiting in this country since at least A.D. 1200. As so often happens, what begins as a necessity develops into a sport and bull-baiting, which was considered essential because the meat was thought to be more tender if the bull had sweated profusely, developed into a favourite English pastime. At one time special by-laws forbade any cattle to be slaughtered until they had been baited and special fields were set aside on the outskirts of towns for this purpose. The bulldog was bred with a flat nose which would not interfere with the bite, protruding jaws for a strong hold, short legs to give the bull's horns the minimum target, and immense weight in order to hang on to its opponent. Its hideous and pugnacious expression has not prevented it from being a childish favourite, as Buster Brown's bulldog companion proved to those who were young in the early years of this century.

Nor has the repellent appearance of the toad hindered it from being much loved. The following anecdote shows both this ugly reptile and the stern Duke of Wellington in an unusually attractive light. One day the elderly soldier chanced on a small boy weeping bitterly and on asking the cause the child began to explain that he was going away to school next day ... not waiting to hear more the Duke read him a severe lecture on his attitude, which was cowardly, unworthy of a gentleman and not at all the way to behave, etc. At last the little boy managed to explain he was not crying because he was going to school, but he was worried about his pet toad, as no one else seemed to care for it and he wouldn't know how it was. The Duke, a just man, apologized to the child for having wronged him, and being human as well as just, took down the particulars and promised to report himself about this pet. In due course the little boy at school received a letter saying 'Field-Marshal the Duke of Wellington presents his compliments to Master x x and has the pleasure to inform him that his toad is well'.

The happy ending of this story is quite unlike the horrid tale of Augustus Hare's youth, and one hopes that few children have been forced to suffer as much as this unhappy boy. His adopted mother (in reality his aunt), pretending to be shocked at his dislike of a new aunt-by-marriage whom she herself detested (since that lady had carried off her brother-in-law, to whom she was attached but, of course, couldn't marry), insisted the boy should give this hated relation what he valued most in the world, which was his pet cat. The poor child, aged about 9, did as he was told and at least had the pleasure of seeing the cat on his weekly visit to his new aunt. But one day for no known reason, and to his inexpressible grief, she hanged it.

Though a number of exotic birds are becoming fashionable again, a far greater variety of bird pets were usual in the past than nowadays. Then selections of little birds were often brought to the door by pedlars who kept them in cages or boxes with little peep-holes, and Jane Taylor tells how one day her mother called her to come and see which she would have among the parrots, macaws, speckled doves with scarlet eyes, linnets, chattering jays and Java sparrows. A number of other birds, particularly the goldfinches and bullfinches, were sufficiently tamed to sit on their delighted small owners' fingers. Bullfinches were unusually good at learning a tune and there are instances of a pair having been taught to sing in parts, a wonderful instance of docility. Bird organs of different kinds were used for teaching tunes, though some people held that this method induced a slightly mechanical style and that the birds sang more feelingly if educated by the flageolet or recorder.

RIGHT: *King James VI of Scotland and I of England with his pet hawk on his wrist, by an unknown artist, and* OPPOSITE: *a small person very much delighted by the visitor who has perched on his arm. The robin has always been a particular children's pet because of its friendliness, and also for its pretty red breast which legend ascribes to the little bird trying to pull the nails out of the Saviour's hands. Reynolds.*

An instance of their remarkable intelligence is the tale of a pair of goldfinches allowed to fly free in an indoor room and outside who, on receiving more food than they needed, went off and fetched hungry members of their own tribe to finish the remains, and on the food allowance being stepped up and up, collected more and more pensioners with the result that their typically English owners felt obliged to leave the windows of that room wide open all winter long.

A similar story is told of a cat given more food than it could eat who collected hungry relatives from afar and ended with twenty pensioners, originally very thin, all of whom always waited for their hostess to eat first ...

The parrot has one outstanding advantage over all other pets, its longevity is such – it has been known to live as long as eighty years – that its owner is unlikely to suffer the unhappiness of losing it. Parrots have always been cherished both for their beauty and affectionate natures (they can never have enough of petting), and also for their capacity of learning to talk. They have been known as pets since remote times but are less popular since psittacosis became a recognized danger, though that disease is known now to be not solely attributable to parrots, but common to many birds.

The Indian conquests of Alexander the Great brought a number of these exotic birds to Europe and there is an early record of a parrot said to speak an 'Indian' language. The best talkers are the grey, red-tailed African parrots who, according to Pliny, were first discovered beyond the limits of Upper Egypt by explorers sent by Nero to search for the source of the Nile. They became great favourites in Rome and were prized not only as pets but as a delicacy for the table – one Emperor went so far as to feed his favourite lions on them. For those which were kept as pets elaborate cages were sometimes made of tortoiseshell and ivory with silver wires, and their beauty and talent was celebrated by more than one classical poet.

As the Roman Empire dwindled the supply of foreign birds diminished, parrots became rare and it was as a great novelty that knights from the Crusades brought back African grey parrots from Cairo. (One knight returned with the even more unusual pet of a small alligator from the Nile.) The bird's retentive memory could prove an occasional embarrassment when swear words learnt at sea from the sailors were used in front of the children, and one knight was extremely annoyed that some underling had taught his parrot to speak in a thick Swabian accent – so very 'non-u'.

Parrots did not become popular pets again until the great age of geographical discovery in the fifteenth and sixteenth centuries, after which a number of hitherto unknown species were brought to Europe and artists delighted to use their tropical plumage as a foil or complement to their sitters' costumes.

The singing yellow canary was at one time an essential item of any correct nursery, and the nightly ritual of covering the cage with a semi-fitted piece of green baize preceded the bedtime of every Edwardian child. Their appearance in Europe dates from the sixteenth century when a ship from the Canary Islands, partly laden with the little birds, was wrecked near Elba, whither a number of them flew. Many were captured by the inhabitants, their gay song made them popular, and they were soon domesticated all over Europe. Their plumage was originally a mixed olive-green, black and yellow, the colours being of varying predominance, and it is the selective breeding by bird fanciers which has produced the popular yellow. In the eighteenth century they were bred extensively in the Tyrol whence travelling salesmen brought them to England. Bewick wrote that 'the importation of canaries forms a small article of commerce ... four Tyrolese usually bring about sixteen hundred of these birds, and though they carry them on their backs the thousand miles, and pay twenty pounds for such a number they are enabled to sell them at five shillings apiece', and adds that the canary, though neither of British origin nor a voluntary visitor, must yet be considered ours by adoption. Today the Australian budgerigars, first referred to by Captain Cook, have supplanted the yellow canaries as prime nursery favourites, and the lovely blues and greens to which they have been bred does much to explain their popularity, and although they have not got the songster talent of the canary they never scream as do some kinds of macaws and parrots. No fewer than 10,000 budgerigars

Little Charles, later the 4th Duke of Buccleuch, is obviously very proud of his pet owl in which his dog evinces great interest. Reynolds.

are sold each year, but amongst the many thousands one became nationally famous. Sir Winston Churchill's inseparable companion was Toby, a mixed yellow and green, who accompanied the elderly statesman wherever he went, much to the distraction of international officials. To obtain the bird's prompt delivery in France required a special passport, a medical certificate from the Ministry of Agriculture, a visa from the French Embassy, an air ticket, and a separate sheaf of certificates, visas and tickets from the corresponding French authorities, who nevertheless always arranged that 'Monsieur Toby' always arrived in time to greet his master.

Owls are such rare domestic pets nowadays that a sensation was caused when two boys at Eton recently raised an owl family in their rooms. Special permission was asked, and of course granted, for the pupils to take certain times off to care for the owlets (who had nested in their rooms and been abandoned by their mother), for special foods to be obtained and so forth, and the incident became front-page news followed breathlessly by the entire nation.

In the eighteenth century the problem of successfully raising an owlet was solved by a little boy in a most ingenious manner. He found his other bird-pets would have nothing to do with it, the little ones being terrified, and the bigger jackdaw and magpie furious: the child figured that the owlet, nocturnal and a mouse-eater, might have more in common with cats, so put it with Fanny and her kittens. Fanny looked suspicious but was disarmed when the owlet snuggled up, and regularly provided both her charges with mice. All grew very fond of each other, their only disagreement was that Blinker, the owl, could not bear to see the young catlings play with a living mouse. He would always pounce down and slay the mouse, then very fairly return it to its captor.

Quite obviously the complaints which would be made now with regard to the unclean habits of animals in the house did not apply to those centuries in which hygiene played a small, and servants a large, part in daily life. Few families in any age would go so far as the one described by Pushkin which brought a bear-cub into the drawing-room to be baited by the household cats and dogs for the amusement of a 9-year-old boy, but squirrels were frequently allowed complete freedom in the house. They were also provided with cages in which a revolving wheel allowed them uselessly to expend their energy:

'Did you ever see a squirrel vent his tiny rage

In turning round his tiny cage?'   *Matthew Arnold*

These would of course be the native red squirrel as the grey was not introduced until about sixty years ago, to the immense disadvantage of the red which has been almost exterminated.

Squirrels were once favourite house-pets and had special cages made for them with a small treadmill inside. John Singleton Copley.

The popular rabbit, recently almost extinct in its wild state, but again reaching pest proportions, is still a favourite pet. 'Orphans', by Sir John Millais.

The familiar bunny in its wild state became almost unknown to a recent generation of children, but the white rabbit continued to be bred in captivity as a pet. It is not always the timid creature it is usually thought to be: two small boys during the last war, feeling that the state of the world called for commando-training, brought up two buck rabbits to be very bold and fearless. Although the animals refused to wear the wooden swords so thoughtfully provided for them, they completely ignored interested cats until they came too close on the lawn, when they would turn and glare. If this did not rout the intruders, as it generally did, the rabbits would charge the cats who always fled from so unexpected a situation.

The once-ubiquitous guinea-pig has been superseded by the hamster. This little animal was first found near Aleppo and a description of it sent to the Zoological Society in 1839, but it was not until 1930 that an expedition to Syria found and brought safely to England a female and twelve young, and it is from this litter that the countless hamsters now in English homes have been bred.

Ponies are most children's dream of a pet but one not frequently realized in urban England, nor are the faithful Neddies of the past often individual friends of the modern child, though many get to know them during summer holidays when donkey rides by the sea or in the country are still one of the attractions. Donkey by name is not always donkey by nature as one child who owned a pet donkey observed with delight: this animal taught itself to open its paddock gate and get into the garden for a change of food. The first time the child found it, and rubbed out the tell-tale hoof-prints before putting the donkey back. The second time the gardener caught it, scolded it sharply and put it roughly back. The third time, the child and his father saw the donkey backing out of a bed trying to erase its prints with the tip of a front hoof! He made rather a mess of his sagacious effort – and a new fastening was put on his gate.

Donkey days come before salad days, as L. P. Hartley once remarked. A donkey ride at the beginning of this century, 'Fin de Promenade' by F. Humbert; and LEFT: *a somewhat simpler version of a later date, Paul, the 2-year-old son of the artist, on a donkey. Picasso.*

127

The briefest description of cherished pets, which in England if the cost of their food and equipment is added to their original price is said to account for 100 million pounds a year, cannot omit one pet who has never cost any rate-payer a penny. The dolphin is not a common pet but one with a long and romantic history. Its origin goes back to the time when Dionysius engaged a vessel to take him to Naxos and, overhearing the crew conspire to abduct him, called on magical powers which changed the oars into snakes, filled the ship with ivy and the sound of flutes so that the sailors, feeling madness coming on, dived into the sea where they were changed into dolphins. Since then they have been thought of as spiritual nomads and have always represented kindness and virtue: they saved Odysseus' son Telemachus when as a boy he fell into deep water and this was why, so Plutarch says, his father had a dolphin engraved on his ring and emblazoned on his shield. They rescued Arion, who was a real person, a poet and a musician, not a god, when on a voyage from Tarento to Lesbos the sailors planned to murder him but gave him a last wish, which was to end his life singing. This he began to do, whereupon a dolphin came beside the boat, took him on its back and brought him safely to shore. Nearly 2000 years ago near ancient Hippo, now called Bizerta, there was a well-authenticated incident of a dolphin coming to the shore and making friends with the children, particularly with one little boy whom he allowed to ride on his back. This, together with other stories of friendships between dolphins and humans, was considered purely legendary until, at the other side of the world in 1955, a similar occurence took place. At Opononi on the coast of Northern New Zealand a dolphin came in to shore and played about with the children bathing, let them handle it and even allowed some of them, particularly one little boy, to ride on its back. Hundreds of people came from all round to see this engaging sight which proved the ancient legends to be true, not mythical.

Most pets are given special names and though goldfishes have not much character even they are recognizable individuals and, like humans, change colour with their health. One child noticed that his fishes' tails had become pale and colourless, and when on enquiry it was found that their water had been changed recently, a scientist present surmised they had 'caught cold', and gave them a dose of antibiotics, whereupon their tails once more became brilliant red.

Some animals have been immortalized by fortuitous names: the mongoose is known the world over as Rikki-Tikki-Tavy and all hedgehogs are recognizable as Mrs. Tiggy-Winkle. Another animal who became famous, but not under its own name, was Sir James Barrie's sheepdog Luath who grew to an immense size and was the original of Nana in *Peter Pan*. Ronsard commemorated in a neat couplet the dog of a royal master, Charles IX, who had had a pair of gloves made from the skin of his dead pet:

'Courte ainsi morte et vive a fait
A son roi service parfait.'

A more modest tribute was paid to a pet in humbler circumstances by William Cowper in the lines

'Though once a puppy, and though Fop by name
Here moulders one whose bones some honour claim.'

The odd fancy that animals might consider their owners THEIR pets was delightfully developed in Walt Disney's *101 Dalmatians* where the dogs, who spoke in undeniably canine voices, took great care of their human pets – a conceit anticipated by Pope some couple of hundred years earlier when he put the following inscription on the collar of a dog he presented to his Royal master:

'I am his Highness' dog at Kew;
Pray tell me, Sir, whose dog are you?'

A sixteenth-century conception of Arion playing his fiddle while riding to safety on a dolphin's back. Girolamo Mocetto.

129

A late eighteenth-century little girl and her doll modelled in wax by Flaxman, probably a portrait of his sister.

RIGHT: *Boucher painted this little girl and her doll, the latter dressed in the adult fashion of 1739. Detail from 'Interieur de la Famille'.*

Their dolls

The doll is among the earliest artifacts made by the human race and has been found in ancient tombs all over the world. Its English and French names give the essential clues to its dual nature: 'doll' comes from a Greek word meaning idol, *poupée* from *pupa* (puppet), and from time immemorial the doll either has been revered as a symbol or used as a plaything.

The dolls of past civilizations were objects of ritualistic and sacred import, talismans or good luck symbols. Many were credited with occult powers and dispensed with a face as it was feared that recognizable features might expose human beings to evil powers. Some were almost flat boards with the arms incised or moulded to the breast, others were mere stumps. The so-called 'paddle dolls' were strips of painted wood with tresses of hair made from strung beads, those with no feet represented concubines who could not run away; others, known as 'answerers', were workers who had to fulfil their

LEFT: *Naked herself, a little girl clutches a severely dressed doll,*
detail from 'Charity'. Cranach. RIGHT: *Here the doll is grandly dressed in close*
imitation of her small mistress, detail from 'Mother and Children'. Renoir.

master's requests, and these were sold very cheaply so that even the
poor could purchase immunity from slavery after death. Some dolls,
particularly those of the palaeolithic period, showed strongly em-
phasized female characteristics and were fertility emblems, of which
the harvest 'corn-dollie', not yet extinct in Europe, is a late survivor.

From a pagan fetish to a semi-religious object was only a short
step and in medieval times dolls were used to illustrate the mystery

plays but, just as most of the fertility idols were considered too dangerous for children to touch, so the elaborately carved Crib figures were too precious, and cannot be considered dolls in the sense now attached to the word – which is itself of comparatively recent date. Its earliest appearance in print is thought to be in the *Gentle-woman's Magazine* of 1751, though undoubtedly it was in current use somewhat earlier, but previously dolls were called 'jointed babies' or 'puppet-babes'. When Sir Walter Raleigh took presents to the Indians in Virginia and they were said to be delighted with the 'babes brought out from England', reference is made to the wooden dolls he gave the natives to amuse them, not to children.

Most primitive tribes made miniature figures roughly dressed like themselves for their children to play with, few little girls have grown up without a doll even if it is only a bone wrapped round with a rag, such as London slum children played with not so long ago and which is now in a museum. Dolls of clay or wood, some with movable arms, were among the playthings buried with children in Ancient Egypt to accompany them to the World of the Dead, and a still extant Roman rag-doll of about 300 B.C. is remarkably like those which continued to be made until World War I. The cloth doll's unbroken popularity in Mohammedan countries is attributed to the Islamic tradition that Ayesha, Mahomet's child-bride, brought her rag-dolls to her new home, just as it was the custom for Japanese brides to take their dolls with them when they married.

Most of the early Greek dolls were of burnt clay but some were of exquisitely carved alabaster or ivory with inset eyes of glass or crystal, and we know how their limbs were made to move by Plato's comparison of a man to a doll and his passions to the cords which caused his movements. There are no pictures to record the love of long-ago children for their 'babes' but little Greek girls seem to have been particularly fond mamas, and when they became nubile they placed their discarded dolls on the altar of the goddess of love. One memorial tablet records this touching request, 'O Aphrodite, despise not my doll's purple neckerchief; I, Sappho, dedicate this precious gift to you'. In a charming letter which Plutarch wrote to console a mother for the loss of her daughter he recalls the incident when the child had begged her nurse also to suckle her dolls.

Few medieval dolls have survived, but an early example can be seen in the museum of Notre Dame in Strasbourg which shows a group of mounted cavaliers, probably somewhat similar to the figures of a *demoiselle* on horseback accompanied by her *valet de pied*, sent by Isabeau of Bavaria to her daughter, a Queen of England when only 7.

The wooden doll became a German speciality from the Black Forest district and varied from a mere stump with roughly painted head to carefully carved models with movable arms and legs, from miniatures easily contained in an egg no larger than a thimble, to big ones almost the size of a child which had their own baby dolls. These, originally called 'Flanders babies', became the popular 'Dutch' (*Deutsch*) dolls, nicknamed Peg-dolls in America, which were the everyday playthings of most children. Charlotte Yonge's favourite, Miss Eliza by name (a prize for hemming her first handkerchief), was a large wooden doll of this kind which continued to be the most common type until gutta-percha, rubber and other compositions began to be used in the last century. Finally even the 'penny wooden' was ousted by cheap celluloid, which in its turn has been superseded by the polythene mixtures of today.

In 1914 a halt was called to the German doll industry and Japanese competition became a new factor in the toy-market. The Japanese girl-doll, who in her own country has a special festival in March (there is another for boys' warrior-dolls in May), had already become a great favourite in the nineties when 'Japonaiserie' was fashionable in Europe, and now the Japanese flooded the market with cheap copies of the Western doll as well as its Oriental counterpart. Today the vast output of cheap plastic dolls from Japan and Hong Kong reaches every corner of the globe.

The china doll, though obviously more fragile than its wooden counterpart, usually had a fairly solid bust attached to a sawdust-filled calico body, with arms ending in white china hands and legs in black buttoned boots. A favourite nineteenth-century style showed a head with round, rosy face and dark hair parted in the centre, fashioned after Queen Victoria at the time of her wedding, another with curls on its brow and neck represented the Empress Eugenie and Jenny Lind was also a favourite model. Most of these were made in Staffordshire factories which specialized in a very high glaze, but in 1850 France produced bisque, a porcelain with a matt finish which permitted a softer, more natural colouring and this, together with its English variant, Parian ware, began to be used for most of the better-class dolls.

Wax dolls have a long and distinguished ancestry. Cheap makes showed wax laid over composition but as early as the sixteenth century dolls' busts were made of well-modelled solid wax attached to stuffed figures of white kid which gave rise to the expression, considered vulgar by past generations but unintelligible to the present, of 'up to dollie's wax' for those who had eaten their fill. At the Great Exhibition of 1851 the Montanari family, now established in London, showed beautifully modelled dolls which for the first time had real hair set into the wax, real eyebrows and lashes and solid glass eyes made by the same firm in Bristol, and in the same 'millefiori' technique, as that used for the famous paper-weights. These caused a sensation: a big export trade in the eyes rapidly developed as well as in the dolls themselves, and Montanari models are now collectors' pieces. Another Italian family, the Pierrottis, who could trace their connection with doll-making back to the twelfth century, were also settled in London, and for a time English dolls rivalled even their French sisters.

Wax was the usual substance of which the eighteenth-century long-clothes baby-dolls were made and several poor, pale, bedraggled creatures still exist, but although they had a period of popularity they were never as much in demand as the fashionably dressed lady-doll. The Edwardian long-clothes doll with its elaborate robes, pelisses and bonnets owed its success partly to the new psychological theories which believed it preferable for the child to nurse an imitation baby than a miniature adult, partly to the rosy-pink wax of which it was made, but chiefly because now it could shut its eyes and appear to sleep peacefully. Although Aristotle describes a doll whose eyes closed by

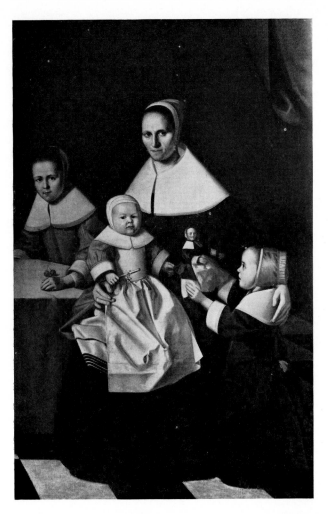

Mother, children, baby and doll, all wear heavy stuff dresses with large snowy white collars. Detail from 'A Family Group'. Michael Nouts.

means of a pulley, and eyes on wires were known in the eighteenth century, it was not until 1824 that a firm in Paris took out a patent for mechanically closing eyes, and they were not in general use until the end of the century, and 'flirting eyes' which moved from side to side were not perfected until much later.

'Such beautiful dolls that will open their Eyes,
You may wash, comb and dress them and not fear their cries.'

But another half a century would pass before 'wetting' dolls would make toy babies even more naturalistic: how shocked those who had disapproved of Montanari's lovely dolls would have been at such a development, for some fault-finders considered the dolls' natural appearance prevented children from using their own imagination – a criticism many educationists today would consider valid.

Mechanical devices for making dolls walk had been known in the seventeenth century: Louis XIV's little son had two performing soldiers made of silver, and in London a man suitably named Merlin made some 'machinery' in his Hanover Square rooms which consisted of two silver dolls about twelve inches high, which walked about, while one raised an eyeglass and the other held a bird on her forefinger. In 1826 an American firm took out a patent and began to manufacture walking dolls, and in the sixties a model was launched under the impressive name of AUTOPERIPATETIKOS, followed in this century by one more modestly christened 'Dolly Walker'.

The first speaking doll was constructed by the same ingenious man who invented the metronome, later a model was brought out by Edison, and a 'phonograph' doll appeared at the Paris exhibition of 1900. By the beginning of the twentieth century most of the beautiful French dolls could walk, talk, say 'Mama' and go to sleep. The firm of Jumeau produced particularly exquisite models with well-moulded faces, swivel necks and pierced ears who were always dressed in the height of fashion though no longer as miniature adults, but rather in imitation of their young owners. Children's clothes had ceased to be exact replicas of their parents' and little girls now wore short skirts, socks and flat shoes – and so did their dolls.

It was not only gentlemen who preferred blondes and most little girls chose dolls with fair hair which curled to their shoulders:

'I once had a sweet little doll, dears,
The prettiest doll in the world,
Her cheeks were so red and so white, dears,
And her hair was so charmingly curled.'

The toilettes of these fashionables were contained in miniature trunks which had a compartment for a 'best' hat in its domed lid and a tray to hold its accessories, and when the young owner went on her annual visit to the seaside she would look anxiously for her doll's small trunk among her mother's large ones. The luggage of one foot high Miss Flora McFlimsey contained not only clothes and bonnets made by some of the most famous *couturiers* of her day, but also monogrammed writing paper, visiting cards, work-baskets, photograph albums and all the impedimenta of a lady of fashion of her day, for

> 'Miss Flora Mc. Flimsey, of Madison Square
> Has made three separate journeys to Paris;
> And her father assures me, each time she was there,
> That she and her friend, Mrs. Harris,
> Spent six consecutive weeks, without stopping,
> In one continuous round of shopping ...
> Nevertheless I have heard her declare
> That she hadn't a thing in the world to wear.'

The upkeep and grooming of such elaborately dressed creatures was the constant preoccupation of any little girl-owner in whose life the dolls' hospital played an important rôle, particularly if she had to pay its charges out of her own pocket-money. Here noses could be re-paired, new eyes put in, new wigs obtained or old ones re-dressed, new bodies attached to beloved old heads, or new heads bought to replace broken ones. All these minor and major accidents of the nursery could be treated at the dolls' hospitals, once so numerous, but now few in number. Like clothes, dolls today are thrown away when damaged, and new ones bought rather than old ones repaired.

Dressing their dolls has always been a favourite pastime with little girls but few have devoted as much energy to it as the young Princess Victoria who, under the tutelage of her beloved governess Lehzen, collected no fewer than one hundred and thirty-two dolls of various sizes, a large number dressed and labelled by herself, all of which can be seen today in the London Museum. Although it might have been surmised that such industry presupposed an extreme love of clothes, no such trait developed in the Queen who later became known for her conservative and sober taste.

Dolls have always reflected the very height of fashion and have themselves played a large rôle in its making. For hundreds of years the dissemination of fashion was achieved by the despatch from Paris of dolls dressed in the latest *mode*, and this practice continued until printed fashion plates and albums took their place in the last century.

One of the earliest-known examples of a fashion doll was in the fourteenth century when the 7-year-old Isabella of France married Richard II of England, and the child-bride was sent fashionably dressed dolls from Paris, some as large as herself so that she could use their splendid attire, others doll-sized for her to play with but which showed how her clothes should be made. The family accounts of the French Royal court in 1497 give the details of a life-sized doll ordered by Queen Anne of Brittany as a gift for Queen Isabella of Castille which at first was considered wanting in elegance and had to be re-dressed before it was despatched. No wonder little girls became fashion-conscious at an early age when not only they but their dolls were newly dressed in the latest style. In 1600 when Henry IV of France was about to marry the young Marie de Medici, he wrote to her saying that 'Frontenac tells me that you wish to have samples of our fashions. I am therefore sending you several model dolls'. The wily Queen-to-be did not make the same mistake as that later royal bride, the Portuguese Princess who arrived to marry Charles II in an outdated farthingale and was ridiculed by the English court ladies dressed in modish panniers. The dolls sent from Paris to Marie de Medici may have shown the Florentine dressmakers the fashionable French cut but the Florentine brocades and Genoese velvets in which the trousseau was carried out caused a sensation in France. These were such a challenge to the local textile trade that a Royal subsidy for the silk mills at Lyons was granted with the avowed aim of making them the most important in Europe. This they rapidly became and Colbert later declared that France would one day be 'the wardrobe of the world', thereby swelling her revenue – which duly happened and Paris has retained her supremacy for over four hundred years: a success based on the most exquisite and refined taste, not on that of the multitude.

Immensely luxurious dolls became fashionable royal gifts in the seventeenth century and vast sums were spent on these useless puppets: no less than 2,000 écus was given for a doll complete with a change of clothes and toilet accessories for Mademoiselle de Bourbon, and the Duchess of Orleans paid even more for a similar gift to the Infanta of Spain whom Louis was about to marry. A beautiful doll complete with a most elaborate wardrobe was presented by the city of Paris to the ill-fated little Grand-Duchess Olga of Russia when she visited France with her parents, and a last echo of this tradition was the pair of dolls given to Queen Elizabeth and King George VI for their daughters when they were in Paris in 1938. These represented Princess Elizabeth and Princess Margaret and were each accompanied by a splendid trousseau contained in no less than fifteen small blue leather trunks with silver fittings.

In the eighteenth century it became popular to have a pair of dolls, one dressed *en grand toilette*, the other *en déshabille*, called respectively *Grande Pandore* and *Petite Pandore* and these fashion dolls, or Pandoras as they were called, became the recognized advertising medium for French fashions throughout Europe. The dolls, usually half-size, were exposed at the Hotel Rambouillet before replicas were despatched to the various courts, and these ambassadors of fashion represented not only the textile trade but all the one hundred and one other accessories for which Paris has always been famous. All Europe looked to the dolls of the rue St. Honoré, invoiced as *les grands courriers de la mode*, to know what was the latest fashion, and even a *précieuse* such as Madame de Scudéry did not disdain to advise on their dressing. So important were these fashion dolls considered that when the various countries were at war with each other special passes were issued to ensure their safe conduct. In 1704 the Abbé Prévost wrote to a friend saying that 'by an act of gallantry which is worthy of being noted in the chronicles of history, for the benefit of the ladies, the ministers of both courts granted a special pass to the mannequin. That pass was always respected, and during the time of the greatest enmity experienced on both sides the mannequin was the one object which remained unmolested'. Such an almost unbelievable act of courtliness

Bess of Hardwick's 'dearest jewel Arbella', Lady Arabella Stuart, was painted when she was nearly two years old, wearing a stiff white satin dress trimmed with seed pearls. Her doll is dressed in a green kirtle and crimson brocade over-skirt.

is indeed worthy of notice, and it is sad to learn that the free pass for the *Grande Poupée* ceased at the end of the first Empire.

The fashion doll was one of the attractions of the annual fair in Venice, and in London its arrival eagerly awaited ... 'Last Saturday the French doll for the year 1712 arrived ... in King Street, Covent Garden' and after being circulated among the court ladies was sent to Mrs. Temple, the dressmaker. Some of these dolls were life-sized so that their fine clothes could be utilized, but the doll itself travelled back and forth between Paris and London dressed in the newest styles on its outward journey, and returning despoiled of its finery.

Fashion dolls were ordered by Marie Antoinette from her famous milliner Rose Bertin when she wanted to acquaint her mother and sisters in Vienna of the latest Paris fashions, and Rose Bertin's dolls

Both the lady dolls so proudly held by these eighteenth-century little girls are dressed in the height of fashion. A lace and flower trimmed taffeta robe, black neck-band and mittens are worn by the doll below. N. Dance.
RIGHT: *Christopher Anstey's small daughter delightedly shows him her new doll's high and elaborate coiffure. W. Hoare.*

became so famous that when she escaped to England she continued to send her annual mannequins to the courts of Europe from London.

It was not only French clothes which the fashion dolls advertised but also the art of the coiffure. In 1763 Paris had an exhibition of some thirty coiffured dolls which showed the latest hairdressing, and Madame de Sévigné had one made specially for her daughter in the country to show her how to arrange her hair. Rose Bertin describes her model for 1777 as having not only a lavish trousseau but 'a very fine wig'.

In the late eighteenth century the English in their turn began to send fashion dolls to America and in 1812 a special convoy guaranteed the safety of the ship transporting the 'latest mannequins from London', which specialized 'in tailored redingotes and sports clothes'.

The last example of fashion dolls was the exquisite *Théâtre de la Mode* created by Paris after World War II which, in a series of miniature scenes designed by leading artists, showed doll-figures dressed by famous Paris *couturiers* in the strangely ill-proportioned post-war fashions.

Among special types of dolls are those which it was the habit of families in India, Persia and Turkey to dress in the finest clothes of their time and to keep as heirlooms. The same custom was followed by at least one English family, the Powells, whose succeeding generations from 1754 to 1912 dressed a doll in the clothes of the period, carefully dating each figure, all of which are now displayed in the Victoria and Albert Museum. In the inventory of Catherine de Medici's belongings after the death of her husband there were eight fashion dolls all dressed in elaborate mourning together with their cost, and Queen Marie of Roumania left two collections of dolls, one a series dressed to represent important personages of her time and the other to record the various peasant costumes then still worn in her country. Among other dolls of particular historical interest are the

LEFT: *A contemporary version of a child with its doll, this time a sailor boy, not a fashionable miniature lady. Maya, daughter of the artist, by Picasso.*

RIGHT: *Looking at what she can never hope to have, a poor little Victorian waif gazes longingly into a shop window full of wax and rag dolls. 'The Toy Shop'. W. Mulready.*

English 'pedlar dolls' which give such a fascinating insight into the requirements of country housewives when a village store was a day's journey away and a village fair an annual event.

In this century a monstrosity came to join the ranks of special dolls, but the 'Kewpie' with its swollen body and inane head made its American creator a millionairess. Another trans-Atlantic new-comer is the 'Bye-lo' baby-doll modelled after a three-day-old real baby and quite terrifyingly lifelike.

Although dolls are a girls' speciality and few boys would confess to playing with them, there have been exceptions. Little Louis XIII was presented with four dolls dressed like the Queen, his mother, and three of her ladies all seated in a carriage, and the Duc de Maine received from Madame de Thianges a life-like wax group including a figure of the little Duke himself showing some of his verses to his tutor Monsieur de Rochfoucauld, together with several other notables, such as Racine and La Fontaine. Francis Thompson admitted he was devoted to dolls and said he fell in love with and dramatized them, calling his favourite after the Empress Eugènie, but did not 'father' or pet them.

Dolls are not often of the male sex though some were made from time to time: little boys in Mameluke costume were fashionable after Napoleon's campaign in Egypt and later small figures in Directorie clothes, patterned on the King of Rome, had a short vogue. Small sailors were moderately successful, and in the last half century the filming of Pinocchio's exploits has made the little Italian manikin a popular boy-doll, but the trousered doll to obtain real success was Miss Upton's Golliwog of the nineties – which strongly resembles the woven Coptic doll of A.D. 500 ... If its black stocking body, mop of black wool hair and boot-button eyes might be considered nowadays a symbol of out-of-date colonialism at least no colour prejudice was involved, and the black Golly was as much loved as the pinkest wax doll. There was even a multi-racial rag doll which had two interchangeable heads, one black, one white, with a tea-cosy shaped skirt which could be turned up or down to reveal either colour and confound any politician.

Their dress

A fragment of an Egyptian fresco shows Ahknaton's two little daughters playing together, naked save for their jewellery and some heavy eye maquillage.

For thousands of years children were dressed as miniature adults and wore whatever was the current fashion. Little Babylonian girls learnt to walk in pleated flounces, half-moon gold pendants and ear-rings, tiny Roman girls in a tunic and jet or amber rings and bracelets, medieval children in floor-length robes with flowing sleeves and long necklaces – all dressed in imitation of their mothers. In the past children were permitted far more jewellery than they are today when even the most indulged teenager would not be given the golden chains of Cranach's young princess, nor the splendid necklaces of coloured beads with which Ahknaton's two small daughters, innocent of all other covering, are adorned. When dressed, these children would wear long garments of fine linen and a wig, just like grown-up Egyptian women, and would own already combs and bronze mirrors for their toilet, as in later centuries little girls were presented with ivory or silver dressing-table sets. Greek girls dressed like their mothers in gaily coloured chitons of wool or linen and sometimes tied their hair on top of their heads in a pony-tail as the young still do. Roman boys wore short tunics and often hung an amulet round their necks, while the sons of northern barbarians copied their fathers' over-dress and leggings. A luxuriant growth of hair was associated by the Franks with vigour and power, so children began to wear their hair long, the boys to the shoulder the girls to the waist, but only very young girls were permitted to wear it hanging free, once a girl was adolescent her head was covered with a snood or veil.

In a modern world dedicated to democracy where rich and poor dress much alike it is almost impossible to realize the immense importance which was once attached to display. Medieval manners considered it as correct to emphasize high station as now it would be thought vulgar. The long robes of babies have always been symbols of rank, and little Princess Elizabeth was so swaddled in a purple velvet mantle with a long ermine train that it had to be borne by two nobles. A man who was rich and powerful dressed his children as grandly as possible: a king's daughter is described as wearing scarlet stockings with a dress of silk and cloth-of-gold, but little peasant girls wore sober-hued homespun. Fine cloth, delicate silks and bright colours clearly distinguished rich and powerful from poor and humble, and the equality of blue jeans lay in the distant future.

The trousseaux of royal princesses were designed as showpieces to reflect the importance and wealth of their countries, and in an age when children were married before their teens no child was too young to be a fashion influence. Edward I's daughter, Margaret, had her own tailor, Roger, when she was 10; little Isabella of Valois was only 7 when she came as a bride to England but her trousseau set a new style which was copied immediately by the court ladies – but what were impossible for them to imitate were the lovely foreign

A Tudor nurse's severe white ruff and high black hat make dramatic foil to the dress of the child she carries. The ermine tails with which the puffed satin sleeves are hung probably denote Royal blood. The feather-trimmed hat is that of a boy though the shoulder ribbons hanging down the back were more often worn by girls. English School, circa 1610.

materials, the murray-mesereon velvets, shot taffetas and beautifully marbled green cloths. How the English husbands must have been nagged by their wives and daughters, and how the English cloth merchants must have fumed! In strong contrast the trousseau of another young bride from France, Margaret of Anjou, was considered so inadequate that a tiremaker was sent to the port where she landed to make her, at top speed some more elaborate costumes, and so we have recorded the first-known name of an English dressmaker, Margaret Chamberlayne.

The ample draperies and trailing skirts which composed medieval clothes were singularly unsuited to children, but suffered by them all until fashions changed drastically in the mid-fourteenth century. The long robe of oriental origin, which in its time had replaced the classic toga, was now abandoned by the male sex for the doublet and trunk hose, and suddenly it became as important for men and boys to have a well-turned leg as it did for women and girls in the 1920's when skirts became knee-high. Girls' dresses no longer swept the floor and although ankle-length were far less cumbersome than hitherto.

The reign of the tailor now began: clothes were intricately cut instead of being clumsily draped, and since they fitted more closely to the figure and used less material they made up for lack of amplitude by elaborate ruching, quilting, slashing and embroidery. Moralists of course were appalled, as they always are at any new fashion, and the Church fulminated in vain against the tight-fitting nether garments and short tunics which some said made the men look like skinned frogs, but which suited the little pages to perfection. A similar fashion revolution took place in the 1950's when coloured elasticized tights for girls were such a success that a pseudo-Florentine effect was given to city streets by hordes of youngsters dressed in skin-tight pants and short jackets, often gaily coloured but, alas, in less beautiful materials and worn with less elegance than their Renaissance prototypes – if with as much bravado.

The small princes and princesses of Florence, Mantua and Urbino were magnificently portrayed by the painters of their time who delighted in the gleaming satins, rich velvets and embroideries of

Two sixteenth-century little
girls differ on coiffure but
agree on wearing as much
jewellery as possible.
A small Medici princess by
Bronzino adds a long chain
and jewelled pendant to her
parure of pearl necklace
and ear-rings.

A young princess of Saxony
wears immense golden chains
wound round her shoulders as
well as a jewelled necklace.
Lucas Cranach the Elder.

their costumes which were clearly intended as illustrations of the wealth and importance of their families. The children themselves were valuable pawns in the complicated game of inter-marriage and power-politics in which the European noble families then indulged with passion. The little girls are shown as sumptuously attired and bejewelled as their mothers, and the little boys imitate in miniature the grandiose doublets, capes and feathered caps of their fathers – but their hair is dressed simply and cut short in a manner still fashionable today.

The children of the great did not always enjoy the luxuries associated with their class: after Anne Boleyn's downfall little Princess Elizabeth's governess pathetically requested that the child may 'have some raiment, for she hath neither gown, nor kirtall, nor petticoat, nor no manner of linen', and the children of Charles VI of France were sent to an institution where they were nearly starved and became covered with vermin. Their half-mad father, in a moment of clear-mindedness, realizing their condition, begged their governess to pawn a gold cup and remedy matters ... it seems a small as well as somewhat tardy gesture of help for the poor children, two of whom later became Queens of England.

In the sixteenth century it was usual for all children up to the age of 3 or 4 to wear similar ankle-length robes, and while they were at the bib and tucker age it was impossible to distinguish the sexes, though the girls' accessories were usually more elaborate and sometimes included two wide ribbons hanging down the back which have never been explained, but may have been vestigial remains of leading strings.

Children's clothes often reflect a past fashion, such as the child's robe which recalled the discarded medieval dress, but in the seventeenth century little boys caught up with contemporary FEMALE

Plain Miss Mockels is justifiably proud both of her tame bird and her splendid crimson dress trimmed with silver braid which clearly shows the back ribbons then so often tied onto the shoulders of children's costumes. She wears multiple bracelets and a fine swag of beads across her chest. Cuyp.

The little Dauphin, later Louis XV, wears a low-necked gown with elaborate sleeves and a trailing skirt exactly like his 'governante's', but his sex is betrayed by his fine feathered hat, so different to the lady's ruffled mantilla. *Largillière.*

fashion and wore much the same sort of dress as the ladies. Largillière's picture of Louis XV as a toddler shows him in a tiny edition of his 'governante's' dress with full skirts to the ground, a wide décolletage and high head-dress. The great moment in any little boy's life was when he could remove the childish robe and appear in breeches and doublet, take off his baby's cap and put on a miniature man's hat. Often a small cloak and sword were added to the costume for pleasure rather than use, and there are innumerable pictures of little boys at this thrilling stage when babyhood is left behind and they attain male status.

> 'Joy to Philip, he this day
> Has his long coat cast away,
> And the childish season gone,
> Put the manly breeches on.' *Charles and Mary Lamb*

*Breeched at last: little Robert Dalzell, son of the 6th Earl of Carnwarth,
is obviously delighted with his fine pink and blue silk knee-breeches
and jacket and gold-braided velvet hat. P. Mercier.*

With the advent of the Age of Reason
little boys were no longer put into
breeches and embroidered coats when
petticoats were discarded, but wore
severe nankeen trousers buttoned high
on blouses sometimes trimmed with
ruffles. Master Frederick Van Diest,
by John Hoppner.
Flat black shoes and white socks, still
symbols of childhood, became fashionable
at the end of the eighteenth century.
The sad little boy hunched up in his chair
was the son of the artist, Boilly.

156

Still skirted and petticoated in the first decade of this century Francis and Christopher Bacon were painted together by Sir William Nicholson.

This habit of dressing little boys in skirts continued for about 400 years and only died out at the beginning of this century. Clear sexual differentiation in clothes is of comparatively recent date and is already on the decline. In the ancient worlds (as today in the Orient) as many men as women wore skirts. It is the industrial West which is responsible for promoting the skirt as a predominantly female garment, a position from which it is fast retiring; but though innumerable girls wear pants, boys have not yet retaliated by taking to sarongs or skirts.

The trousers now indiscriminately worn by both sexes first became popular at the time of the French revolution when these plebeian garments, hitherto used only by sailors and uncouth northerners, became the signature of the rising middle-classes. Little boys when they left off petticoats were no longer put into knee-breeches and embroidered coats, now associated with the hated aristocrats, but given long nankeen trousers buttoned on to frilly shirts.

LEFT: *Looking down on the world with the unchanging curiosity of the child, a small girl peeps round the corner. She wears a scalloped apron over her short, full skirt and a lace embroidered cap. Crivelli.*
RIGHT: *Her hair freshly out of crimpers and held back by a star-trimmed ribbon this fat young person looks prepared to dispute anyone's authority. Her embroidered bodice has full over-sleeves of a bold design. Detail from a 'Family Group', by Licinio.*

At the end of the eighteenth century little girls at last began to wear more childish clothes and to be less hampered by fashion. Corsets had always been inflicted on them, and though few races were such ardent advocates of tight-lacing as the Circassians, who forced their daughters from the age of 8 or 10 to wear a broad leather girdle which was not removed until the bridegroom cut it off on the wedding night (no wonder they tended to marry young), most girls wore a corset of stiffened cloth or leather laced up the front. Nor have boys always escaped such discomforts and many small beaux wore rigid stays under their stiff-bodied coats – one small Duke found his so irksome that, not surprisingly, he beat his tailor. Before the French Revolution girls had been constricted in panniers and boned bodices as their predecessors had been in farthingales and ruffs, but now a new fashion arose which, although it was first launched in England, owes a great deal to Jean Jacques Rousseau. Among the many

Hundreds of years separate
these three little boys, all
of whom wear long hair
without loss of manly prestige.
LEFT: *Federigo Gonzaga, son
of Isabella d'Este, was
painted when he was ten with
his hair in a shoulder-length
page-boy bob. Francia.*
BELOW: *A prince of Saxony
wears a jewelled wreath at
a dashing angle
on his fair head. Cranach.*

Renoir's son Jean, now famous as a film producer, used to have his curly red hair tied back by a ribbon when he went out to bowl his hoop in 1898.

II—C.F.C.

161

abuses against which he campaigned was the fashion of corseting, as he did with much success against swaddling, for he maintained that the growing child's body should be allowed to develop naturally. He would have approved the later dress-reformer who advocated 'Fizical helth thru clothes' even though he might have been startled by the spelling.

These new dresses, innocent of bones or stiffening, together with the fashionable flat slippers, composed a costume eminently suitable for the young, who were now allowed to wear their hair short and straight instead of frizzed and elaborately dressed. This is a fashion which truly can be said to have crossed the Channel from north to south, for Reynolds was painting his young sitters in plain white

LEFT: *Her hair on top of her head, large gold ear-rings and a high waisted dress make the daughter of the artist, Guèrin, a miniature of her fashionable 1st Empire mother.* RIGHT: *Line Campineanu wears an off-shoulder dress and long gloves like any grown-up bourgeoise of the 1890's. Manet.*
OPPOSITE: *The simple white muslin dresses with coral or azure sashes, often with flat slippers to match, which became fashionable in the late eighteenth century, composed one of the prettiest costumes ever devised for the innocent young. This little girl was soon to learn the 'dirty devices of the world', for she was Anna Isabella Milbanke, later the wife of Lord Byron. John Hoppner.*

Pairs of sisters in the nineteenth and twentieth centuries: the lace-frilled dresses of the early Eighties have sashes placed at the fashionable low waist-line and show the white socks and black strap shoes worn by most children. 'Rose et Bleue', by Renoir.
RIGHT: *In the Twenties 'Maud et Raymonde' wear miniature copies of their mother's waistless, ultra-short dresses. The eldest still has long hair but the youngest has succumbed to fashion and has had hers cut short. Van Dongen.*

muslins and coloured sashes when Madame Vigée le Brun's daughters and her friends were still wearing boned satin bodices. There is a world of difference in the spirit as well as the fashion in which these eighteenth-century children were depicted, and the studied elegance of Nattier, the fictitious pathos and cloying sweetness of Greuze's girl-models, contrast strongly with the healthy youngsters that Reynolds and Romney painted with straightforward delight. To be dressed *à l'Anglaise* became the 'highest ton', for the muslin dresses, though plain, were as clear a sign of status as had been the elaborate

satins of the past, since originally this new material came from the Indies and was both fragile and costly. About a hundred years later when Sir John Millais painted 'Little Miss Muffet' in the fancy dress of mob cap and mittens, muslin had become the usual material for little girls' dresses and only continued to have snob-appeal when it was elaborately hand-tucked and lace-edged.

Little girls' troubles with their clothes were by no means over: in time the simple dresses went out of fashion, tight bodices and elaborate sleeves returned, ankle-length 'trowsers' were worn under short skirts by both boys and girls and were not always, as one might reasonably surmise, a pair of pants, but sometimes merely a pair of ends tied on with tapes at the knees; only later when the crinoline came in were they proper drawers. Thackeray describes a child going to a pantomime in a brougham where there was not sufficient room for both her and her mother's crinoline and she was obliged to wear hers straight up over her head! Quite small tots barely escaped the bustle and although they did not boast real pillows tiny dresses were made with extra padding below the waist to support a vestige of back drapery. This was the style worn by Alice when she went through the Looking Glass, in contrast to the crinoline in which, a decade earlier, she had gone to Wonderland, and which eventually led to the charming fashion for sashes. A collection of these with their matching hair-ribbons was an important part of a *fin de siècle* little girl's wardrobe, which would contain silk ones from France with elaborately made-up bows and fringed ends, kept in a special box and carefully ironed each time before they were worn.

The utter impracticability of children's clothing during the last half of the nineteenth century would be hardly credible were it not so well documented. Every conceivable and unsuitable material – velvet, plush, silk, sarsanet – was tucked, ruched and trimmed with lace and fur. No wonder someone enquired

'How many poor animals must we employ
Before little Charles can be dressed?'

Already in the time of Napoleon III the *Journal des Modes* gave considerable space to juvenile fashions which continued to reflect the increasing elaboration of grown-up styles. But the intricate dresses of the seventies and eighties did have one great improvement, their skirts were short, and these when worn with ankle socks and strap shoes allowed children more leg freedom than they had had for centuries. Renoir's adorable little Charpentier sisters and a host of other small sitters show to perfection this fashion which may have been cumbersome and was certainly unhygienic, but perhaps because of the artist's palpable enjoyment, seemed exactly right for small girls. But Renoir's love and consideration for children was such that he

Two seventeenth century little girls of a comparatively humble family wear ankle-length dresses with white fichus. The elder has an apron tied over her skirt and a necklace of beads, and both have their hair caught up with ribbons. Louis le Nain.

rounded the corners of furniture and chimney-pieces to lessen the bumps and he and Mme Renoir never went to the theatre without paying a flying visit home during the interval to see that their young ones were safe and sound.

In the sixties the length of skirts was a clear guide to the age of a girl and a magazine categorically announced what was correct: at 4 the skirts should be just under the knee, then from 8 to 14 the hem

168

The Belleli sisters both wear the white pinafores with ruffled shoulder straps which were popularized by 'Alice' towards the end of the last century. E. Degas.

Until recently aprons were a part of every child's wardrobe: the little son of Sir John Thynne, builder of Longleat, clutched a rattle when he posed for his portrait in a stiff costume covered by a curiously creased apron. Attributed to Eworth.

should descend at regular two-yearly intervals until at 16 (the age of puberty) it should be only two inches above the ankles.

Although the apron, like the corset, is considered an essentially feminine accessory it too has not been unknown to little boys. Folded aprons such as the one seen in the portrait of Sir John Thynne's small son were often tied over childish robes, and not long ago French boys all wore a black alpaca apron at school until they were 12 (see p. 55), when they were promoted to a suit with a starched turn-down collar and a large Lavallière bow.

The schoolboy's knickerbocker suit with its belted jacket and bulging trousers fastened below the knees hailed from America but soon became the French boy's daily wear until he left school and was promoted to manly trousers. Julian Green tells the sad story of a boy imploring his parents for a pair of long pants and being reminded that his uncle had bicycled to his first employment still wearing his boyish knickerbockers.

It has always been usual for a distinctive costume to mark the student, from the medieval scholar's robe, of which an echo still persists in contemporary academic dress, to the Blue-coat boys with their monkish soutanes, and the Eton boys whose striped trousers and shrunken jackets recall the Regency dandy. The French schoolboy's dark blue hooded cape was one of the familiar sights of French towns until, like the Eton boys' top hat, it proved a casualty of the last War. Now the children in French streets, like those in other countries, are a confetti of blue, red and yellow pullovers allied to dark pants. The English blazer dates only from the last century and unfortunately was adopted by girls' schools, whose inhabitants all too often resemble those pupils of St. Trinian's whom Ronald Searle has made world-famous. Indeed the reaction of foreigners to our educational methods is often of astonishment evenly divided between the brutality meted out to the boys and the ignoble appearance forced on the girls.

To look different is a torment to a child, conformism is born in their bones. Even the angelic 'Old-fashioned Girl' suffered agonies when she realized her white muslin dress with its blue ribbons, which she had thought most elegant and proper at home, was entirely unlike her town friend's smart pink silk with its tarlatan tunic.

> 'How proud we are! how fond to shew
> Our clothes, and call them rich and new –
> When the poor sheep and silkworm wore
> That very clothing long before;
> The tulip and the butterfly
> Appear in gayer coats than I.
> Let me be dressed as fine as I will
> Flies, worms and flowers exceed me still.'   *Dr. Isaac Watts*

Fanny Price in *Mansfield Park* was afraid her grand cousins 'could not but hold her cheap when they found she had but two sashes and had never learned French'. Lady Ritchie (Anne Thackeray) recalls her and her sister's dismay at a party given by Dickens's children when they found their young hostesses flounced in white silk and shod in white satin when they were wearing tartan sashes and austere black shoes, and the aesthetic dress of little 'Monna Givronda Cimabue-Brown' was mercilessly criticized by more conventionally clad children. Henry James was only 10 when Thackeray met him in New York and, amused by his tight, brass-buttoned jacket, said in England he would be called 'Buttons', but this incident so impressed young Henry that the oddness of Americans is a theme which runs through all his novels. Romilly John was known to pray that his mother, the admired Dorelia, would come to the school sports wearing 'proper' clothes and not the graceful costume which his father's portraits had made famous. It is an adult soul indeed who is prepared to be different from its neighbours: one Eton master explained the school's system of allowing each boy a room of his own from the day he arrived, as a means of developing the boys' personalities, for he said 'all humans are gregarious, one has to teach them to be individuals.' At a recent round-table conference of teenagers, convened by adults to ascertain their views on school-uniform, they one and all voted for it because, they said, it made them all look alike.

Some mothers thought otherwise, and the habit of dressing boys as miniature soldiers and sailors is of long standing. The success of

The fashion for sailor clothes dates back to the early nineteenth century:
here the young Grimpel wears an 1880 French version, complete with a striped
vest, white tapes and a sailor hat. Renoir.

Winterhalter's portrait of the little Prince, later Edward VII, in a sailor suit, plus hundreds of pottery and china copies, tipped the scale in favour of the small sailor who is still occasionally to be seen. The apogee of this fashion was during the first decade of this century when the little royalties of Europe, boys and girls alike, were dressed in sailor suits with large straw sailor hats ignominiously held on by elastic straps, and parents of lower rank dressed their children like the little aristocrats who, of course, were playing at being democrats. The sailor blouse was usually worn by girls teamed with a pleated skirt, and this costume under the name 'middy-blouse' became the popular school dress of American girls before World War I.

An alternative to the sailor suit was the kilt: Queen Victoria's liberal use of plaid in the furnishings of Balmoral and in her children's clothes had resulted in a rage for Scottish tartans. Small boys' dresses were often of plaid velvet, and children of both sexes wore the kilt, the boys with smart little jackets and glengarries, the girls with unsuitable blouses and Highland tam o'shanters with pompons instead of plumes.

A third choice, for boys only, which arrived from America early in this century was the Buster Brown suit. This consisted of a single-breasted jacket with a flat round collar and floppy bow and straight short pants, accompanied by a round straw hat and the new Buster Brown shoes which 'correctly shaped the growing foot while giving style to the shoe'. Buster's straight short hair and fringe was also widely copied. He is now a treasured memory of the over-50's, unfamiliar to the young, but another imaginary little boy of the same period set a fashion which still exists: Peter Pan collars are worn today.

The Edwardian mania for long hair caused great suffering to little girls who were expected to wear theirs as long as it would grow and were taught that to be able to sit on one's hair was a most admirable feat. How many must have heard the lines:

'It is not to tease you and hurt you, my sweet,
But only for kindness and care,
That I wash you, and dress you, and make you look neat,
And comb out your tanglesome hair.'

The horrors of rag-curlers which covered the head with a series of hard knobs and made it impossible to lie down comfortably became the Western torture-equivalent of the Eastern bound feet. Generations of children endured nightly discomfort, not without complaint, though few rebelled as violently as the child who later became the famous author, Gyp. A born rebel, she had already announced that fallen angels intent on perdition had taught people to pierce children's ears, a practice which at that time was considered good for the eyesight. She persuaded a boy-cousin to cut off her porcupine hair-curlers. This he did and afterwards described her as looking like a happy frog – but she was far less happy when her parents' reaction had made itself felt. The American bob, or Dutch cut as some called it, came to the rescue of little girls just before World War I, hair was worn shorter and the hideous curlers disappeared.

Fashions, like politics, were undecided during the thirties, but the vogue for simplicity in the twenties had eliminated a mass of unnecessary detail from the child's wardrobe. At the end of World War II a major fashion change took place, as drastic and far reaching in its influence on juvenile, as the French Revolution had been on adult, fashion. This came from the New World where children were, and are, of far more consequence than in Europe. The clothes of teenagers began to assume a hitherto undreamed-of importance. Not only were the practical requirements of growing children seriously studied for the first time but their likes and dislikes were also considered. The dungarees worn by workmen in the Old World were adopted by teenagers in the New as a symbol of freedom, and blue jeans became their daily wear. Sartorial sex-habits were reversed, instead of small boys and girls both wearing skirts they now dressed alike in pants. As usual it was the headgear, always intensely susceptible to fashion, which gave the clue: when both sexes had worn identical skirts the boys were conspicuous by their wide-brimmed hats, trimmed with ribbons and feathers, which far outclassed their sisters' more modest bonnets; now the rôles were changed and girls grew their hair long and evolved elaborate hair-do's while the boys went in for simple crew-cuts.

Mademoiselle Romaine Lacaux wears a grey over-dress with a white muslin blouse and black sash, and her hair is held back by a ribbon to reveal jewelled ear-rings. Renoir.

Not only were play-clothes created for children but more elaborate fashions were designed solely for the new teenage customers. Modern parents who deplore the early sophistication of their young may like to be reminded that the problem is an old one, at any rate in America. Anthony Trollope (European and prejudiced in the 1830's) and

*Some eighty years
later Susan Mayor
posed for Christopher
Ironside in
a work-a-day version
of navy tunic and plain
white blouse with
a head-band but
no jewellery.
Bernard Buffet painted
Kiki in the Fifties in
an embryo over-blouse,
vestigal pants and no
ribbon in her hair.*

The Child and the Rose: Ford Madox Brown painted this serious little girl holding a rose, her earnest face framed in a halo hat, her dress embroidered in pre-Raphaelite flowers, and a double necklace of amber round her throat. RIGHT: *Lady Diana Manners when a child, holding up her long dress with one hand and offering a rose with the other. Sir James Shannon.*

Louisa M. Alcott (home-grown and kindly in the 1860's) both give thought-provoking accounts of the upbringing of girls, many of whom at the age of 14 not only aped their elders' clothes and coiffures but also their flirtations, and attached great importance to boys when dolls would have seemed more suitable playmates (though it is worth remembering that their Tudor ancestors at that age would have been married). Such independent manners took some time to reach English shores where girls were incarcerated in schoolrooms until at least 17, but the post-war teenage fashions crossed the Atlantic as

fast as any jet. Not only did European children take to blue jeans and play-suits *en masse* but their parents did likewise. Instead of the child being dressed unsuitably in a miniature replica of his parents' elaborate costume, the parents – almost as unsuitably – now wore casual clothes like their children. If in the past it had been difficult to distinguish boys from girls in identical long skirts, children now were often hard put to it to tell mother from father. The aim of fashion was no longer to establish, but to abolish, differences of sex and class, and the trappings of privilege were exchanged for proletarian anonymity. Had the Victorian poor worn as little as the children of the rich do today they would have been the recipients of charity. When 'Each had a round hat, each had a muff, Each had a new pelisse of soft green stuff' how could any little girl imagine her near descendants would be content with pants, pullover and pixie hood? and that 'Sunday Best', which once upon a time prevented even slum children from playing in the streets, would be unknown? Yet the days are not long past when in order to go out into the garden they donned

The pelisses, muffs and broad-brimmed hats of Kate Greenaway's five sisters recall the costume of Lady Caroline Scott, whose portrait so charmed Walpole that he said one 'longed to catch her up in one's arms and kiss her'. Reynolds.

such garments as Mary Clive describes, a once 'best' but demoted, rose-trimmed velvet hat lined with pleated satin, and a broderie-anglaise collared coat. Nor can little boys believe, if ever they are told, that once upon a time not only did they all wear white gloves and Eton suits (if they were spared Lord Fauntleroy's velvet) for parties, but that their hair was put into curlers for such occasions.

Dressing for an Edwardian party was a lengthy affair for little girls which entailed long hair being washed, brushed and tied with ribbons, the putting on of clean frilly knickers and petticoats, long black stockings or clean white socks according to age, black or bronze slippers held on by cross-over elastic, and last of all a complicated dress probably made of muslin trimmed with ribbon-threaded Irish crochet mounted over stiff silk.

The 'babies' balls' which Hannah More so greatly deplored and the Edwardian fancy-dress parties were far more splendid affairs than those held today and involved sums of money which would be inconceivable now. Children have always loved to dress up their dolls, their pets and themselves, but many a male infant whose

Getting ready for a party in the early eighteenth and late nineteenth centuries: LEFT: *A little girl gives a lingering look at her reflection while her mother arranges her hood. Chardin.* RIGHT: *Nurse ties a tippet round the head of a child dressed in a short crinoline of broderie anglaise. James Hallyer.*

appearance as Cupid in a wisp of chiffon and a wreath of roses was recorded by painter or photographer has lived to regret his mother's choice of costume. That little Louis xiv was once similarly dressed, or undressed in public, that Baby Charles, James i's son, appeared in nothing save a short green tunic and a pair of gauzy wings, and that Edmund Kean made his stage début as a Cupid when he was 4, could be of only small consolation.

To be dressed up, even if only with a hat, gives obvious pleasure to this naked youngster self-consciously posing for his portrait by Reynolds.
RIGHT: *Two little girls, having discarded their doll, delight in dressing up their kitten by the light of a candle. Wright of Derby.*

Master Crewe, son of the Earl of Crewe, delightedly posed for Reynolds in youthful imitation of Holbein's portrait of Henry VIII.

186

Prince Arthur of Connaught,
aged 5, was dressed as
a miniature Guardsman,
complete with bearskin and
rifle, when Winterhalter
painted him in 1855.
Sir William Rothenstein
painted three of his
children splendidly
disguised in Oriental robes
as the Princess
Badroulbadour and
her attendants.

Pierrots have abounded in all ages: Fragonard's portrait of this adorable little boy dressed as a pierrot contrasts strongly with RIGHT: *Picasso's 1929 version of his son Paul similarly attired.*

In the past a large number of children's portraits showed them in costume because, as an eighteenth-century artist somewhat unkindly explained, fancy dress supplied 'the interest which might otherwise be wanting in half-formed features'. Such a view would meet with no approval today when the interest of the child itself is paramount, and children are more often recorded in their play than party clothes.

Their food

The British breakfast table in 1962.

No one detail of a child's life has altered more during the centuries than its meals. The amount and variety of a modern child's diet would be inconceivable to his forebears of a few generations ago, and the pampered little Westerner who sits down to a breakfast of cereal, fruit-juice, bread, butter AND jam can have no conception on what frugal fare his predecessors survived.

Food is not only an infant's first necessity but also its earliest source of pleasure, from the moment when, if it were a Byzantine baby, its gums were rubbed with honey. The immense importance of food in a child's life is reflected in the myriad heart-rending accounts of its lack, hunger seems to have been the main concern of most children and its satisfaction their first cause for thanksgiving. All too often there was remarkably little to be grateful for, nor were the lessons in gratitude always given in a manner to recommend them: when the young Wesleys forgathered at breakfast and from the age of one were admonished, while raising their hands for family prayers, to 'bear the rod without loud weeping' there was more to weep over than to eat, for breakfast consisted of broth without bread, and supper was the same. Until the last hundred years the European child of the lower classes subsisted mainly on bread, gruel and dumplings, with only occasional meat and very few vegetables, a diet singularly deficient in vitamins. As late as the nineties children in London's East End were nourished almost entirely on bread, so that 'to take the bread out of anyone's mouth' was tantamount to condemning them to starvation. How healthy in comparison sounds the food of the early Sumerian children who enjoyed beef, mutton, dates and milk and with their bread ate cheese, as well as the clarified butter which still forms a major item of the diet in the East; or that of the Egyptians in the time of the Pharaohs with their carraway cakes, their favourite dish of goose roasted over live embers and the figs, melons and cucumbers so well remembered by the Israelites. They ate with their fingers as Arabs do to this day, and were allowed to lick their fingers as modern children may not, but afterwards had water poured over their hands using jugs and basins almost exactly like those of Victorian times.

Tied up with bows and lace in the eighteenth century the young Archduke Ferdinand eats a biscotta similar to those still made today. Anton Raphael Mengs.

During the Middle Ages there was no fresh meat during the long European winters for, as there was no fodder, all cattle were slaughtered in the autumn, and though Sir Hugh Platt assured the housewives of his day that powdered beef could be kept for two or three months if wrapped in dry cloths and put in a tightly closed cupboard, it can hardly have been good for the young. The inventory of a typical larder in a great house might contain 'the carcases of twenty oxen, and fifteen pigs, of herrings eight thousand, of dograves seven score, twenty pounds of almonds, thirty of rice, six quarters of salt', but such a diet of pickled meat and salted fish eaten with bread was wholly unsuited to children. The enormous number of carcases which had to be cut up for the large number of persons in a lord's household caused elaborate rules for carving to be laid down, and these became an important item in a young page's training:

'Courteous he was, lowly and serviceable,
And carved before his father at the table.'

In those days milk was considered fit for infants only until their foreteeth were grown, butter was used as a cure for growing pains or with the addition of sage as a purge for the blood, and as honey was the only known form of sweetening most houses kept their own skips of bees. Little fruit was eaten as it was thought to induce fevers and not until much later was it found to be a preventive of scurvy – a discovery which gave the appellation of 'limeys' to English sailors who, scurvy-free, used to suck limes and lemons on their journeys in the East.

Vegetables were not only scarce but unpopular and either pickled or used for soups, 'greens' were not yet the hated bugbear of a child's dinner and salads were rarely eaten. No wonder we hear of antiscorbutic juices being administered to an entire household, from the Countess of Bedford to her maid Mrs. Abigail, at 2/6 each.

One sixteenth-century child, sent early away from home to some noble household, appears to have fared unusually well and writes to his parents that for breakfast he had 'bread, butter and fruit ... to dinner greens or porrige ... on fish days, bread and milk – if fish be reasonable in price we have it fresh if not salt fish, but well soaked, and beans and peas. Some drink small beer, and a few have wine well watered. Afternoone we have bread and raisons, almonds, apples, cherries. For supper, salad with salt, and oil and vinegar, boiled mutton with dry prunes or roots and herbs. Or gallantine of minced meat – sometimes pancakes – and cheese and nuts. We have as much bread as we will, and other things sufficient for nourishment, but not for the filling of our bellies'. It must have been quite a belly which could deal with so much and still feel the want, and it must have been an exceptionally lucky child, for it enjoyed fruits and vegetables at a time when most people suffered from ills due to their lack.

By the seventeenth century the situation had improved and the inhabitants of great country houses began to enjoy many luxuries more commonly associated with the present than the past. Their vegetables included artichokes and asparagus as well as root vegetables and greens, lemons and oranges supplemented home-grown fruit; in the store-cupboard were Westphalian hams, figs, raisins, dates and a good selection of spices. If the pickled food was not always to the taste of a child the still-room would contain candied flowers made into conserves, honey from the comb, preserved fruits and water flavoured with rosemary. If he was good he might be allowed a sip of the home brews made from elderberries and dandelions or the cowslip wine which 'if kept in a cool place will last till cowslips come again', and small beer was usual for dinner. Children were early taught to take part in the preparation of such luxuries and many a little girl could make ratafia before she could spell it. Sweets as we know them did not exist, and though sugar-dolls were known at the time of Leonardo da Vinci, they were rarities. Most sweetening was still done by honey, for sugar, brought from the East in the shape of a hard cone which had to be chipped and pounded, was extremely expensive. It was not then refined in such a manner as it is today when the taste is left but the food value is extracted. These were subtleties which would not be known until later, when in the Welfare State of the twentieth century 'sweets' became the bugbear which pickled foods had been in the past, this time attacking the children's teeth with caries, not their skin with scurvy.

Zoffany painted the family of John, 14th Lord Willoughby de Broke, in 1771, gathered round one of the newly fashionable tea-tables, complete with tea-urn, tea-cups and a bowl from which one of the children hopes to scoop a goody.

In the eighteenth century tea and coffee began to be imported but they were expensive and subject to a high excise duty and so remained a luxury enjoyed only by the rich until well into the nineteenth century, when Henry James deplored those 'little pale carnivorous coffee-drinking ogres and ogresses who prowl down for breakfast' in the hotel. In the meantime fashionable ladies began to acquire elaborate equipment for the new meal of 'tea', a dwarf tea-table became an important part of their household furnishings, fine silver pots, jugs and kettles began to be made and special sets of china for each member of the family were brought by East Indiamen from the Orient. Swift mentions the 'Doiley' napkins then used, an appellation

During the first decade of this century Sir William Orpen painted William Nicholson, his wife Mabel, and their four children in their Bloomsbury dining room. The eldest son is now the famous abstract painter Ben Nicholson.

not yet demoted into a non-U expression by Miss Mitford, but merely the name of the linen draper who first produced them. Children were occasionally invited to this essentially grown-up observance, as the picture of Sir Willoughby de Broke and his family charmingly illustrates, but the splendid spread of a nineteenth-century nursery tea-table was still in the future. How puzzled not only the children but their parents must have been at the mathematician who, when asked if he took cream in his tea, replied yes, 'because the globular particles of the cream render the acute angles of the tea more obtuse'.

'Jockolate' also became popular in the eighteenth century though it was not until the late nineteenth that the nursery cup of cocoa

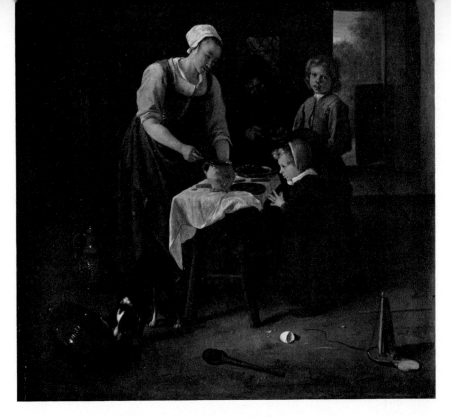

Grace must be said before a meal even if it consists only of little more than a slice of bread and a pitcher of water. J. Steen.

appeared, a beverage which owed its origin to a new method of extracting the pure cocoa essence from the surplus butter content of the cocoa bean. This discovery allowed the former to be made into cocoa powder, later mixed with either milk or water, while the latter formed the basis of our now familiar 'chocolates'. Hitherto when children craved for 'sweets', 'What Katy did' was to offer them such goodies as a bar of cinnamon to chew — even the common 'boiled sweets' are barely centenarians.

Such luxuries as tea and coffee were prerogatives of well-to-do homes and in the schools quite other conditions prevailed. Charles Lamb, when a pupil at the Foundling Hospital, wrote the following description of the food ... 'while we were battening upon our quarter of a penny loaf – our crug – moistened with attenuated small beer, in wooden piggins smacking of the pitched leathern jack it was poured from ... our Monday's milk porritch, blue and tasteless, and the pease soup of Saturday, coarse and choking ... the Wednesday's mess of millet repugnant (we had three banyan to four meat days in the week) ... our half-pickled Sundays, or quite fresh boiled beef on Thursdays (strong "caro equina") with detestable marigolds floating in the pail to poison the broth ... our scanty mutton scraps on Friday – or rather more savoury, but grudging portions of the same flesh, rotten-roasted or rare, on the Tuesday (the only dish which excited our appetites, and disappointed our stomaches, in almost equal proportions!)'. Banyan days were when no meat was eaten, a word derived from a sect of devotees in some parts of the East Indies who never taste flesh.

Other institutions offered similar meals where dumplings, gruel, watered-down milk, bread with cheese OR treacle, and suet pudding were the main ingredients with meat only once or twice a week and vegetables strikingly absent. Even the boys of such famous schools as Winchester and Eton complained with almost equal reason of their diet and all remained hungry – taking with them to school the now-vanished 'tuck-boxes', a wooden, iron-bound box filled with goodies from home (and of which the owner alone had the key), and spending

A seventeenth-century table is laid, the meal is ready and the little girls appear with their over-skirts prudently turned up in front against accidents.
Detail from 'The Family Dinner', by Matthieu le Nain.

their pocket money at the tuck-shop on extra food. One little boy who, when asked what he would like for dinner, replied 'roast duck and apple tart', was told by Lord Holland that 'if all decisions you make are as good you will be a wise man' – but few schoolboys were given the chance to display such incipient wisdom.

Oliver Twist is but the best known of thousands who wanted 'more'. By giving a personality to the deprived child and for the first time making a child the central character of a novel, Dickens brought the plight of children to the notice of thousands who would otherwise have remained disinterested and undoubtedly did much to alleviate the lot of the young. Nor was it only in the homes and institutions of the poor that malnutrition was rife, for the stodgy meals of the rich, though more filling, were almost entirely devoid of the necessary vitamins and their insufferable puddings as unhealthy as they were unappetizing. English children rarely, if ever, enjoyed such a variety of delicacies as those Madame de Ségur describes at a children's picnic – 'hare pâté, daube en gelée, potatoes with salt, ham, shrimps, prune tart, cheese and fruit' ...

With the development in the nineteenth century of an affluent middle-class society immense meals became a sign of success and vast quantities of heavy food were eaten. Turkey, 'plumb' pudding (which originally contained meat) and mince pies were already popular dishes which Martha Wilmot and her 'chicks' introduced in the late 1820's to the foreign ambassadors at the Viennese court, delicacies then unknown in Austria. A menu which consisted of 'a noble round of boiled beef, a turkey, a boiled ham, pheasant pie, sausage rolls, scalloped oysters, and Stilton cheese, pale ale, sherry and negus, with fruit, cheesecake and greengage tart' gives point to the following exchange between mother and child:

'Mama, why mayn't I, when I dine
Eat ham and goose, and drink port-wine?
And why mayn't I, as well as you,
Eat pudding, soup and mutton too?'
'Because, my dear, it is not right
To spoil the youthful appetite'.

Undoubtedly such indulgences would inevitably lead to those stand-byes of the nursery, water-gruel and bread soaked in milk, if not to castor oil, Syrup of Figs, or ipecacuanha if a cold was feared. Such disagreeable medicines are as unknown to our pill-fed children as the horrors of stiff calves-foot jelly, wobbly blancmanges and sago puddings (tapioca was worse), which made convalescence a purgatory.

The child's meal-times have changed as much as his diet. Until the last century breakfast was an early snack and the important meals were dinner and supper. In the Middle Ages, and up to the end of the eighteenth century, children rose at five, dined at eleven and supped at five or six, but as artificial lighting became more general meals were taken later, breakfast became a more solid repast, and afternoon tea filled the long gap between luncheon, which was the children's dinner, and their evening meal, which was usually a bowl of bread and milk. Dry bread and milk was all that Charlotte Yonge had for breakfast and supper in her small squalid nursery, which was also the maid's work-room, except for the three winter months when porridge was substituted for the breakfast bread and milk. As for eggs, ham, jam and other goodies, no one dreamt of giving them to children. Even a twentieth-century child of well-to-do parents was given a meagre diet, Forrest Reid recalls he had nothing but porridge and bread and butter for breakfast, and potatoes, butter and milk for supper.

The revolution at the breakfast table began in America where packaged cereals began to be promoted in the nineties, but did not reach England until 1904. Wheat was the first favourite and remains so today, corn-flakes and puffed rice did not arrive until the twenties, and the pre-sweetened foods, such as rice crispies and frosted flakes which were developed in America during the forties, were not imported into England until all war-time restrictions were ended in the fifties. Together with cereals came the American habit of taking a glass of fruit-juice each morning which was facilitated by the enormous increase in citrus farming and by swift transport. These, together with a glass of milk, form an ideal meal for a child and the familiar egg nowadays more often appears on his supper tray than on the breakfast table.

A similar important revolution took place in infant feeding when new scientific methods, plus the increasing output of new dairy countries such as New Zealand, made dehydrated milk a commercial proposition and infant foods composed of this commodity, packed in sterilized tins, cut down the rate of infant mortality in a quite startling manner.

In most children's memories it is the delight of TEA which looms so large: even Enid Starkie, who complained so bitterly at the squalor of the fish-balls and shepherds' pie which alternated for school-room supper (cook being more concerned with pleasing the 'master' than the nursery folk), admitted that GORGEOUS teas were provided with toast made over the nursery fire, limitless butter and jam, and plain but always huge home-made cakes.

The cook from whom could be coaxed such splendid tit-bits as a slice of bread spread with dripping is a comparatively recent figure in the life of the child. Until the latter part of the eighteenth century men provided most of the household staff, there were laundry and dairy maids but few women below stairs until Tom-in-the-kitchen was finally ousted by the female sex in the nineteenth century. The girls who then entered domestic service formed a floating population which changed frequently as they left to be married, but during their term of domestic service they learnt enough of cooking and house-keeping to serve them well in their own homes. It is this immense and varied school of experience which has been lacking for the past several generations of young mothers, and has led to the tin-happy housewives of today who in a world of plenty buy food from which much of the essential goodness has been lost. The increase of bad teeth in the last century owing to processed and sweetened foods brought about the adoption of the tooth-brush, at first called the 'tooth-preserver' since its daily use was expected to prevent all de-composition. What would those early users of the new invention think of the 'Dento-matic' electric toothbrush of 1962 which cleans teeth automatically? and of which in its first year no less than ten million pounds' worth were sold in America.

'Give me a piece of your tart', two urchins defend their dinner from the demands of a negro boy. Murillo.

Few houses now have a comfy cook in a cosy kitchen from whom children can beg tit-bits, and another source of 'extras', the after-dinner visit to the dining-room, has also vanished. The ceremony of bringing the children down to dessert was once an important moment in their lives for which they were washed, combed, curled, and dressed in spotless clothes. They were then exhorted to enter the dining-room quietly and to remain motionless until given a biscuit or a sip of wine as a reward for their good behaviour. After a taste from her mother's glass Jane Carlyle, aged 4, once said 'Mama, wine make cosy', a remark as truthful but more engaging than most of Jane's recorded sayings. One visitor who thought children always a bore, declared that 'at dessert they were bad enough, at dinner the deuce', but probably most children disliked the whole affair just as much as the guests. Margot Asquith recounts that one of her clearest recollections is that of this alarming ritual, when her grandfather's chair at the head of the table marked the end of her voyage up the room, where that pompous person, his pink face surrounded with white hair and a halo of smoke, would recite with apparent pleasure 'The Owl and the Pussy Cat' and at the appropriate moment put the ring from his cigar on her finger, repeating 'Said the Piggy I will'.

The enormous family dinners of Edwardian days were usually announced by a gong which stood in the hall: Sunday luncheon was inevitably a large round of beef with Yorkshire pudding and two vegetables, followed by another pudding (steamed or suet), or a pie: dinner began by the first course of soup preceded by an immense pile of plates and was served at the table from a huge tureen, the grown-ups first and the children last. But the ample food of the well-to-do did not penetrate far in depth of population and nearly half a century after Oliver made his memorable request a high proportion of children in industrial areas were still subsisting mainly on bread and jam, with the result that rickets, bad teeth and stunted growth were commonplace, and it was not until the advent of cheap tinned foods that the diet of the poor improved. This new form of food, un-wittingly sponsored by Dr. Johnson who once proclaimed 'every-body loves to have things which please the palate put in their way without trouble and preparation', was usually canned meat from Australia. At the end of the century this began to be imported in large quantities and quickly proved popular, but another form of tinned food, evaporated milk, gave disappointing results. Although the children to whom it was given appeared to grow and look well, their vitality was reduced, and to everyone's horror infantile scurvy reappeared. This caused so much concern that a national scheme for providing extra milk for children was launched and proved spectacularly successful. The factory children between 12 and 14 who were given milk at breakfast and supper grew four times as fast as those who did not have it, and the absolute importance to the young of a 'pinta-milka-day' was definitely proved. It was not always appreciated. Not all said,

> 'Thank you pretty cow that made
> Pleasant milk to soak my bread,
> Every day, and every night,
> Warm, and fresh, and sweet, and white.'

The young Grants detested it, so their father stood over them in his dressing gown, a whip in his hands, and administered a sharp cut if anyone baulked at drinking his breakfast ration, a method hardly conducive either to a good digestion or a future liking for the beverage.

There was still some time to elapse before it was realized that a child raised on cow's milk also required extra vitamins from fruits such as oranges or black currants, and although a bill had been passed in 1906 authorizing money to be spent on food for needy school-children, it was not until the middle of World War II that steps were taken to feed all school-children, whether in need or not. The far-reaching results of that wise legislation are evident all around us, the children in Britain are taller, heavier and more robust than ever before, and some years ago the Ministry of Health could proudly announce that malnutrition had ceased to be a national problem.

Behind this miracle stand several individuals whom all children should revere: among them Sir Henry Peek, who believed it useless to give education to the hungry, so to the school he built in the 1870's he added a kitchen, the first ever attached to a school, and provided hot meals for all; the enlightened school inspector who realized the school's high standard of work was brought about by the bodily vigour of the scholars and wrote urgent reports bringing this matter to the attention of the Ministry of Education; Mr. James Pascall who gave back some of the fortune he had made by selling sweets to children by providing breakfasts for hungry schoolboys in Southwark; and above all those wise and visionary statesmen, Mr. Rab Butler and Lord Woolton, who at the beginning of the last war put the needs of the children first and saw that even in the country's most difficult moment the rationing system ensured no child should go hungry. Yet nearly 2,000 years before them a similar system had been sponsored by the Athenian city fathers who in the first century A.D. worked out an alimentary scheme which gave special allowances to children ...

Tied up with a practical napkin the 'Enfant au Verre' grasps an implement in one hand. Derain.

INDEX

The artists and subjects mentioned in captions to the illustrations do not appear in this index, but can be found in the list of illustrations at the beginning of the book.